Healed

Healed

Richard Daly

paternoster
Lifestyle

Copyright © 2001 Richard Daly

First Published in 2001 by Paternoster Lifestyle

07 06 05 04 03 02 01   7 6 5 4 3 2 1

Paternoster Lifestyle is an imprint of Paternoster Publishing
P.O. Box 300, Carlisle, Cumbria, CA3 0QS, UK
and Paternoster Publishing USA
Box 147, Waynesboro, GA 30830-2047
www.paternoster-publishing.com

British Library Cataloguing in Publication Data

A catalogue record for this book is available from the British Library

ISBN 1-85078-406-X

Cover design by Compudava
Typeset by WestKey Ltd., Falmouth, Cornwall
Printed in Great Britain by
Cox and Wyman Ltd, Reading, Berkshire

Contents

Preface

I would like to thank the many who submitted their testimonies and stories of healing all in the one desire to encourage others. To those who gave their support through prayers and encouragement during the progression of the book. To Herbert Griffiths for his timely editorial advice and guidance.

To the Paternoster Publishing editorial team for their vision and commitment in the process of producing this book.

To my wife Maxine and son Ryan, for their love and care in so many ways.

Most of all I give thanks to God. In him lies the power to heal; it is to him that this book is ultimately dedicated.

Richard Daly
July 2000
(richarddaly@yahoo.com)

Introduction

It was during the summer of 1998 as I sat at a church conference listening to various people share their testimonies of healing, that the idea of this book was born. The subject of the programme presented was, 'God is Still in the Healing Business'. I sat enthralled together with the three thousand attendant audience as each testimony was shared. Such was the intensity of the testimonies revealing the anguish and emotional struggles that had been encountered, that no mention was made of the fact that this scheduled programme had gone overtime by over an hour. The congregation was engrossed.

It made me realize how much interest there really is in hearing the personal accounts of people who have overcome their struggles and who can testify to the power of God in their lives. There still lies an interest in the true experience of faith in action. Such true stories have a way of giving us hope in whatever our personal challenges may be. We are reassured that God is still able to perform the extraordinary within the life of the ordinary. The God of the Old and New Testaments is still the same God, and what he was able to perform during those biblical times, he is more than able to perform in our lives today. He is 'the same, yesterday and today and for ever' (Heb. 13:8).

This book, therefore, is dedicated to the awesome power of God, who in his wisdom, deals with his people in ways that are at times above human understanding, but always result in what is best for us. Each chapter contains personal accounts of people who as a result of prayer have experienced healing in their lives. Such stories are based upon proven evidence where medical examination can confirm that a healing occurrence has taken place whether it is in addition to conventional medicine or over and beyond any prescribed treatment. In all accounts, sincere and genuine prayer by the individual and through the prayers of others, is the common theme.

There may be some who will question the sensitivity of a book containing only stories of healing, given the many who feel they have not received healing. In face of this objection I have recognized that healing embraces much more than just the physical, but the emotional and mental. Perhaps most importantly, I have also included accounts where such types of healing never occurred at all, but rather an acceptance of the condition resulted in the greatest healing of all – a spiritual healing. Such an experience happened to me.

It was during the eighth month of my nine-month stay as a missionary in the Marshall Islands that I awoke one day with a severe headache and stomach pains. Before I had left my home in England, we were warned during orientation of some of the diseases that could be caught in a tropical climate. I had taken all the necessary precautions and was at a loss to understand how I'd got sick. During the next two days these symptoms got worse. I developed jaundice and extreme tiredness and eventually had to go to hospital. It wasn't long before the doctor was able to confirm that I had Hepatitis. I was told that Hepatitis is a highly contagious disease that affects the liver and causes jaundice. The laboratory tests later confirmed Hepatitis A. It would take me between six to nine months to recover. I remember my initial response being one of disbelief; as far as I was concerned God had sent me here as a student missionary to teach English and I was determined to complete the remaining last crucial weeks.

By the next day the reality of this illness became apparent as the headaches became more severe, and tiredness turned to total exhaustion and constant vomiting. My urine turned brown, eyes yellow, and my already slim frame was loosing weight rapidly. I had to be isolated from the other missionaries while the principal of the school made the necessary arrangements for me to return to England.

During those two days on my own I was able to open the Bible and meditate on the word of God. Beginning from Genesis I read every account of healing possible. I would pause to reflect on the promises of God, specifically noting the ones about healing (see Appendix 1 and 2). I read and re-read them, taking note of every word and the promises of answered prayer.

During this time a married couple who were also missionaries and managed a smaller school at the other end of the island came to our campus. Upon hearing of my illness they came to visit me. Bob, who was an American, had contracted Hepatitis the previous year. He was ill for six months. Ana, his wife, was from Fiji. Both had now developed strong immunity to this illness. They offered to take me to their home. I gladly accepted. During the next two days with them they prayed ceaselessly. I continued reading, studying and praying. At this point I strongly believed that God would bring about my healing. After every prayer session I would go to the mirror to see if my eyes were returning to their normal colour and constantly checked my urine. I had confidence that God was going to cure me, and quickly.

The next day I awoke and, as has become my custom, I went to the mirror. I looked at my eyes . . . total amazement, no trace of jaundice! I checked my urine . . . it was clear! That morning I had a humongous appetite for food; in the afternoon I played a round of volleyball and went swimming – no exhaustion, but a resurgence of energy! An illness that should have lasted from six to nine months, ended within just one week. I knew that this could only be explained as a direct result of prayer.

After spending just five days with Bob and Ana I returned to my campus. As a leper to the priest I presented myself to the doctor for examination. He marvelled at such a quick recovery. The following day was Monday and I was back in the class teaching.

Although I encountered a physical healing, the spiritual experience I received then was more rewarding. It still remains a source of strength for me to be reminded that the same God can perform such wonders in my life today. It is my hope that this book will be an inspiration to you as you take comfort in the words of the Psalmist; it is he 'who forgives all your sins and heals all your diseases, who redeems your life from the pit and crowns you with love and compassion' (Ps. 103:3-4).

Chapter 1

Anything Too Hard for the Lord?

With man this is impossible but with God all things are possible. Matthew 19: 26

Nothing is too hard for the Lord. As Paul declared, 'He is able to do exceedingly abundantly above all that we ask or think' (Eph. 3:20). The conditions of time, place, ability, circumstances, and all others that could possibly be named, upon which our performance is based, have no bearing on God. He is not limited in action or restrained by the conditions that limit man. The only restraint on his power, the only thing that can disable him, is lack of faith through prayer.

This was evident on a number of occasions from the responses given to Christ's healing miracles. There are no fewer than five consecutive healing stories in Matthew chapter nine. It was after the healing of two blind men, when Matthew 9:32 describes a possessed, dumb man who was suddenly placed before him. The multitudes closed in, keenly fixed on what Christ would do. The demon was cast out and the dumb man now began to speak. The response of the people was divided. Whilst the Pharisees proclaimed that he 'casts out demons by the prince of devils', others exclaimed in wonder and amazement, 'Nothing like this has ever been seen in Israel' (Matt. 9:32-33).

Today the response to healing through prayer is still divided. There are many who will always doubt the power of God, but to the one who believes, prayer becomes the 'hand of faith that unlocks heaven's storehouse where are treasured the boundless resources of omnipotence'.[1] For the believer, prayer becomes the secret of spiritual power. The challenge for us is to listen and become enthralled to the truth that whatever difficulty we are faced with, we need not fear because God's response will always be 'Is there anything too hard for me?'

Jo Ann Wray learnt this infallible truth when her eighteen-year-old contracted a terminal illness.

'On Tuesday, July 3 1990, Dr Forrest walked in and announced, "Michael has testicular

---

[1] White, E.G., *Steps to Christ*, Ontario: Pacific Press Ass., p. 95.

cancer. His left testicle must be removed immediately. Is Thursday or Friday best?"

'"Cancer? Mike has cancer?" The ugly reality tore at me. Mike's face was bloodless. He squeezed my hand as I helplessly patted his. Mike had waited weeks before telling us of the swelling. He thought he'd hurt himself on a canoe trip. Cancer never entered our minds, but now, it stared us in the face with all its terrors.

'We called friends and family asking for prayer. Every night in bed my husband, Roger, and I held each other and cried. We hoped. Maybe the surgery would get it all. Maybe he wouldn't need chemotherapy. Maybe somebody was wrong. But they weren't.

'We needed something to anchor us. Turning to the Bible for comfort, I read Isaiah 58, and the lifeboat we needed surfaced on our sea of fear. The words of verse 8 became a living promise to our family: "Then shall thy light break forth like the morning, and thine health spring forth speedily." We held to that promise tightly the whole time Mike battled the cancer.

'The first surgery went well. Next came a full set of CT Scans. The news wasn't good. Mike needed chemotherapy.

'At the Oncologist's office, Dr Vicki Baker sat across from the three of us and explained the treatment for the tumours. "Tumours? We thought the tumour was removed during the surgery." Roger voiced our shock. Mike's hands trembled and I heard him gulp hard. I barely contained my desire to scoop him up in a smothering hug. Dr Baker gently said, "Mike's cancer has spread to the lymph nodes, several large tumours are in his lower abdomen, and over thirty sizeable spots of cancer on his lungs." When we asked his chances of recovery, the answer was softly delivered, "Less than 20 per cent." More was said, but all I heard was "less than 20 per cent". We cried all the way home.

'When we pulled in the driveway of our home, we sat sobbing, as Mike held our hands over the back seat. Later, we learned testicular cancer strikes about one per cent of the adult male population in the United States. Sixty-five per cent of those stricken learn the cancer has already spread by the time they see their doctors. Those statistics didn't bring any comfort. I kept asking God, "Why Michael? Why does he have this terrible disease?" I didn't get an answer to my questions, but I did sense God's love surround our entire family.

'Mike's first week of chemotherapy started July 16 at St John's hospital in Tulsa, Oklahoma. Given three powerful chemo drugs and four blockers daily, the process took four hours. Roger and I watched the nurses insert the intravenous needle and begin the treatment. Mike slept deeply. We sat at the foot of his bed and prayed as never before. The side effects of those drugs were terrifying and seemed even worse than the cancer itself. The list taunted me: loss of hair, lowered resistance to infection, loss of appetite, nausea and vomiting, mouth sores, possible damage to other organs from the drugs, and a real possibility of never being able to father a child due to total loss of sperm production. Only God could help Mike and us through this.

'The weeks passed. Roger was frustrated and angry. He hates feeling helpless. I agonized, wanting to take the cancer myself, so Mike wouldn't have to suffer. We managed to maintain a semblance of normal family life. Mike continued working when he could. College was put on hold. The school reserved his scholarships and sent cards filled with prayers and scripture promises. We were surrounded by prayer: prayer from friends, from family, from strangers, from all different denominations, from Canada, from Mexico, from coast to coast of the United States, and even from Belgium. We felt the serenity and power of that prayer. Of course we still had ups and downs. Mike would be fine, then boom! The effects of the chemo would crush him. We tried to protect him from unneeded stress, like worrying over college preparations. That could wait. Yet we tried hard to treat him normally. I still yelled at him to clean his room. He and his big sister, Amie, still had sibling fights. But now we loved more. We

hugged more, laughed more. We felt the short-
ness of life and savoured each moment.

'Slowly, we learned that his grace is sufficient
in every situation. As the news had grown
worse, there came a night when I knew I had to
really trust God with Mike's life. I'd spent the
day weeping off and on over the whole situation. Why Michael? What would I do if he died?
I fell to my knees at the foot of the bed, laying
my head and arms on the quilt. Tears rained on
though I felt dead and dry. I choked out a
prayer, "Lord, please help me. I'm willing to
hear your heart. Help me." A deep sense of
peace embraced me as if God himself held me
against his chest. I could almost hear the warm
comfort of his heartbeat. "Lord Jesus," I prayed,
"whatever your plans for Mike's life, whatever
happens, I trust you." There was no outward
change in Mike's condition, yet a deep inner-
confidence resided in all our hearts that we
couldn't explain.

'Mike's hair fell out in hunks, so he went to
get "buzzed". He came home bald, and announced he was starting the "Jean-Luc Picard of
the Starship Enterprise Look". I could handle
that. However, weeks later, as he and I sat in the
kitchen, talking and laughing, I suddenly realized he had no eyelashes! At birth his lashes
were thick and long. Now they were completely
gone. I bolted into the bathroom and shut the
door behind me. Turning the water on full force,

I held a towel over my mouth and sobbed deeply. Right then I realized I could never fully understand what he was enduring to get well. He was my baby, and I couldn't keep his pain from him.

'The second five-day round of chemotherapy came in August. At LaFortune Cancer Centre, new x-rays were taken. Dr Baker put the first set of x-rays on the light board and she turned to us. "Look. Here's the first x-ray on Mike's lungs. See all the spots of cancer?" She pointed then started to cry, the tears sliding silently down her cheeks. I was sure it was more bad news. "What's wrong?" I asked. "No! Nothing's wrong! Look! Here's today's x-ray. All the lung cancer is gone already. This isn't from the chemotherapy!" Her voice was filled with conviction. "This is a miracle! I don't get to see miracles often, but this is one!" Mike broke into a big, beautiful grin. Right there and then we praised and thanked God.'

Mike now attends Friends University in Wichita, Kansas. Still totally healed after nine years, he's full of life, and works as a Network Administrator at a local Christian-owned business. His blood tests and CT Scans have been totally clear since November 1990.

From this whole traumatic experience, not only was Mike healed, but for Jo Ann it led to a deep spiritual experience. 'Now I understand the work of the cross of Christ far better than before', says Jo Ann. As a mother, her first reaction to the news of Mike's cancer was to want to take it herself so he wouldn't have to endure it. God did the same thing for us. He looked down from heaven and saw mankind being destroyed by the cancer of sin. His compassion and love for us compelled him to come down from heaven and take on the sin of the whole world in his own body on the cross. There is nothing too hard for God. Nothing.

'Then the word of the LORD came to Jeremiah: "I am the LORD, the God of all mankind. Is anything too hard for me?"' (Jer. 32:26-27.)

March 1995 became a time of disaster and discouragement for Sue Peel and her husband Earl. Pneumonia ravished Earl's one operative lung. Two other varieties of the disease attacked quickly, and in addition Earl was diagnosed with active Hepatitis C. It was when he was in intensive care for two weeks, totally dependent on a ventilator for life, that Sue encountered an all-powerful, all-wise God.

'The doctors' reports kept coming like shards of glass. "He has emphysema." "We think he has tumours on his lung." "We've been unable to wean him from the respirator." "He can't live for long on the respirator, the lung's too weak." I was bombarded with decisions I couldn't make. "Should we resuscitate?" "Is he an organ donor?" Well-meaning friends offered to help me begin making arrangements. Overwhelmed is too weak a word!

'Doing all I'd been taught, I surrounded Earl and myself with deep Christian praise music. In a commandeered doctors' consulting room near the Intensive Care Unit (ICU), I searched for and spoke out hundreds of promise-filled scriptures. For innumerable hours, I prayed with all the intensity and strength I could muster. I even got loud and yelled at Satan. Yet Earl continued to atrophy and weaken. With his decline came discouragement and fear. Despair followed, bringing a spiritual fog that forgot all the miracles I had ever seen, that forgot the incredible evidence of Christ in our lives.

'One day, on returning from a quick trip to the house, as I walked laboriously towards the hospital entrance through a rather serene area with several small trees lining it, I was stopped. Just one word was spoken – "Listen". I obeyed. First one little wren chirped, then another gave out a small trill. One by one, a philharmonic of birds joined together in a precise and crystal clear harmony. That song went deeper than all the praise I'd ever heard. I stood listening in silent tears, oblivious to those passing by. In that song I heard, "If I can orchestrate this infinite beauty, I can do what is needed for

Earl." I repented from my "works" and simply believed.

'Three days later, Earl was moved to a regular room, minus the ventilator. He walked out of the hospital one week later. Within five weeks of being released, he returned to his job as a long-haul truck driver. Today, over two years later, my husband is still with me, still on the job and still giving glory to the Infinite One.

'Each day the prayer of my heart was

Father, no matter what I see, feel or think, you are God. If healing comes, you are God. If healing is never manifested, you are God. Your Word is truth and it says that you are Love. As Sovereign Lord, whatever you choose to do in this situation, there can be no other reason or motive for it than love. Open my eyes to understanding, open my heart to accept. My desire is for you to be glorified in me and in this situation. Please reveal to me any steps you would have me to perform to participate in your response. Amen.

God didn't give Earl new lungs. He didn't take away all the other conditions that Earl was diagnosed with. What he did do was bring Earl through that near-death crisis and has given him better respiratory health than he has experienced since childhood. A greater vision of who God is was what led

Sue to really believe that our disappointments are God's appointments.

Prayer was never too far away from the lips of Joan Clayton. Upon hearing of the tragic accident of her son Lance, seriously burned in an explosion, she cried, 'Help me Lord, I pray for strength and strong faith to weather this storm. I believe that you are faithful. I believe that you are with Lance right now, and that you will bring him to total victory! Nothing is too hard for you!'

'I almost fainted when I looked at Lance. The skin on his arms was hanging by strings. His face was horribly blistered, red and swollen. The cotton t-shirt had melted away and only bare, raw burned skin remained on his chest. It was almost more than I could bear, but I felt my faith rising. The thought in my mind was: "God, this isn't too hard for you!"

'Amidst the tears and prayers, I began to hear the story of the accident. Lance was filling a tractor with butane gas on my Dad's farm, which was 30 miles from town. A blinding explosion occurred. His face and arms were exposed to the full impact of the explosion. Lance, being on fire, rolled over and over in the dirt. That alone, could have caused severe infection. He ran to the tractor, started it up and amidst the pain, anguish and shock, started driving everywhere and nowhere. Lance could hear himself screaming. He drove at break-neck speed, going through pastures and barbed wire fences. He came upon a large earth tank, filled with water. He stopped the tractor long enough to submerge himself. This provided some relief and prevented further shock. Lance jumped back on the tractor and after a few miles came upon a little country store. The store-owner's car would not start either. A man "just so happened" to drive up. He also "just so happened" to be a medic who had been in the Vietnam war. He put Lance in his pick-up and raced to town at 100 miles an hour.

'The doctors were calling from the emergency room door. Both Connie, his wife, and I hurried to the door.

'"This is Dr Jenn," our family doctor was saying, "He has just recently moved to our town and 'just so happens' to be a burn specialist."

'"He's a mighty lucky boy," Dr Jenn was saying, "He could have been blinded so easily. He could have been burned much more severely. I cannot tell you right now that there will not be scarring, but we can treat him here. I don't even think he will need skin grafts, but we must guard heavily against infection."

'I thought of Lance rolling in the dirt and jumping in a dirt tank that was full of all kinds of germs, but I reaffirmed my stand. I would not waver. "God, this isn't too hard for you!"

'At 3 o'clock on the morning of the third day, my husband and I suddenly awakened from a sound sleep and jumped out of bed:

'"We've got to get to the hospital right now. Lance needs us!" The Lord was leading us into intercessory prayer that was so desperately needed at this hour.

'We arrived at the hospital to find Lance wrestling and agonizing in pain. We donned our masks and gowns and began to pray as earnestly as we knew how. After about twenty minutes, all three of us looked up at the same time. There was a calm, a peace, a stillness about the room. Lance was sleeping peacefully in a deep sleep. We could feel and sense the presence of ministering angels. God had answered and the crisis had passed.'

Today Lance has tall, handsome sons of his own. Joan's words of gratitude were 'I thank God all over again that nothing is too hard for him!'

'I know that you can do all things; no plan of yours can be thwarted' (Job 42:2).

Chapter 2

In the Master's Hands

'Like clay in the hand of the potter, so are you in my hand…' Jeremiah 18:6

It must have been a strange request for Jeremiah… 'Go down to the potter's house, and there I will give you my message.' God had been using these practical illustrations in order to convey various messages to Jeremiah for his people. No doubt on this occasion Jeremiah was probably wondering, 'What does God have in store for me this time?'

So according to the biblical account in Jeremiah 18:1-6, Jeremiah went down to the potter's house, and saw him working at the wheel. The potter took the formless grey lump of clay in the cup of his hands and began to turn the wheel. Jeremiah marvelled at how, in a short time, the potter was able to shape and form the lump of clay into a vessel of beauty.

Maybe at that time Jeremiah thought 'This must be the message: God can create something beautiful from something undesirable', but as Jeremiah watched closely, suddenly (v. 4) 'the pot he was shaping from the clay became marred in his hands…'

Jeremiah watched as the potter took the marred vessel, and squashed the clay together again into a formless heap. 'Could this be the message?' Jeremiah thought. Judgement has now come upon my people and surely we will be destroyed!

Then something unexpected happened. Just when it seemed the potter had finished his work, he picked up the clay once again and 'formed it into another pot, shaping it as seemed best to him' (v. 4). When it seemed there was no hope, the potter began his work all over again. The message: 'Can I not do with you as this potter does? Like clay in the hand of the potter, so are you in my hand.'

Sara is a true example of one who was re-shaped and moulded by the hands of the Master potter. Her story is one that reflects her strength of character. She struggled with discouragement and hopelessness, but was carried forward by her personal trust in God, emerging as one who had indeed been re-formed by the mighty hand of God.

Talking to her mother back home in the Welsh hills was important to eighteen-year-old

Sara Edwards. Moving to the heart of the city of Liverpool from the tiny village of Caeathro, Gwynedd, was a big jump and she had made a point of ringing home regularly.

On that Wednesday night, 4 February, Sara had mentioned that she had a sore throat. 'I'll be all right soon,' she reassured her mother. But at 3 a.m. she woke suddenly in her room and was violently sick. She told fellow student Katy Elders how she felt. When at 7 a.m. Katy went to check on Sara she found her collapsed on the floor and burning with fever. Bundling Sara into the night porter's car, she raced with her to the university sickbay.

It soon became clear that Sara was seriously ill. Delirious with fever, she developed a reddish-purple rash. By half past ten that evening her condition was finally diagnosed: bacterial meningococcal meningitis, the killer disease that strikes like lightening and claims over two hundred victims every year. An ambulance rushed her to Liverpool's Fazakerley Hospital. When Sara's parents arrived at her bedside around 1 a.m. they could barely recognize her. Her entire body was covered with purplish-black bruises caused by the bleeding of her capillary vessels as septicaemia spread to attack her vital organs. Her mother Margaret thought she looked as if she had been beaten by a club. Already Sara's heart had twice stopped beating. The doctor told Margaret and her husband Dewi that their daughter might die within hours.

Sara regained consciousness briefly. She had recently studied meningitis and knew how important it was to keep the circulation going, to prevent body tissue dying. Sara asked her parents to rub her hands and legs. All night long they did as she requested.

The following day Sara suffered a respiratory failure and was rushed to a life-support machine. Then on the Sunday her liver and kidneys failed and she was transferred to Dialysis at the Royal Liverpool University Hospital, her own medical school. As Sara lay in a coma, specialists told her parents that there was only a 5 per cent chance she would live. What they did not say was that they had never seen such an advanced case of meningococcal meningitis. A nursing sister was more direct. 'I'm afraid Sara is leaving us, you know,' she said, gently. But Margaret drew on the stubborn resilience she shared with her daughter. 'That can't be right. She'll live. You'll see. She will live.'

News of Sara's fight for life spread throughout the hospital and medical school. Members of the University's Christian Union to which Sara belonged set up a 'prayer chain'. So many joined the round-the-clock prayers in one student room that the meeting spread to other rooms in the hall of residence and to the student union. Prayers were also said at the nearby church where Sara worshipped.

Sara's condition continued to deteriorate. Her lungs failed. Against all odds she hung on. But her damaged blood vessels were no longer supplying blood to her legs and gangrene was about to set in. On 15 February, eleven days after Sara had fallen ill, Dr Anthony Gilbertson, director of the hospital's intensive care unit, asked the question he had dreaded having to ask. With her parents' permission, Sara's legs could be amputated below the knee. Otherwise, he explained, the gangrene would poison her within days. 'I'd rather have Sara here with no feet than somewhere else with both feet,' Margaret said. 'Go ahead.'

Once behind closed doors Dr Gilbertson struggled to hold back the tears. Of all the operating decisions he had had to make, the amputation of an eighteen-year-old's legs was the most difficult. Margaret walked alongside Sara as she was wheeled to the operating theatre. As Dr Gilbertson manned the life-support machine sending air into Sara's weakened lungs her eyes opened and closed. Margaret looked down at those beautiful blue eyes and thought, 'She's still there, my angel is still there.'

Three hours later, doctors had amputated both Sara's legs below the knee.

For two weeks Sara's life hung in the balance. Her already trim eight-stone body withered to five and a half stone. Newspapers told of her fight for life. Hundreds of well-wishers sent cards, flowers and stuffed animals. The 'prayer chain' now stretched around the world as more than 100,000 people prayed for Sara's recovery.

At last her vital signs stabilized. On 5 March, four weeks after she had been admitted to hospital the unbelievable happened: Sara opened her eyes. She'd survived. Dr Gilbertson summed up the feeling of the entire staff: 'We have a miracle in this hospital once a year. This year Sara is our miracle.'

Confident that Sara would have the strength to cope, Margaret and Dewi told her about her legs as soon as she regained consciousness. She had seemed to understand, but she was still being weaned off her medication and soon forgot everything they told her. 'Why am I here?' she kept asking. 'What's wrong with me?' Again and again her parents would gently repeat their explanation.

It was three days before realization suddenly dawned on Sara. Very agitated she asked a nurse to telephone her parents. At 5 a.m. on March 8, Margaret and Dewi arrived at her bedside.

'They've done something with my legs,' an astonished Sara told them. Once more, they explained what had happened.

'Which leg has gone?'

'Both,' they replied.

Barely audible, Sara whispered, 'Both? Both my legs?'

That was when Sara's second battle began: the battle to believe she still had a life worth living. Initially Sara felt happy just to be alive. A non-stop parade of visitors helped lift her spirits. She was the hospital's most dramatic success story and she was surrounded by love. Then the bubble burst.

On 8 April, on her first visit to the artificial limb centre, she shuddered at the ghastly looking steel and wood 'pylons' she would have to wear. An elderly amputee limped over and said carelessly, 'Well, dearie, your dancing days are over!' Sara broke down in tears. There were more blows to come.

On the May bank holiday, Dewi and Margaret took Sara out to Liverpool's Albert Docks for the day. They were a family again, out on a holiday excursion. But as Dewi pushed Sara's wheelchair laboriously over the cobblestones she began to notice people staring at where her legs should have been. She saw the same look of horror and pity flash across every face. *I'm out in the big world now*, she realised, *and I've got no legs. I can't stay cocooned in the hospital forever*. Again Sara's tears flowed.

Back in the ward Sara wept all night for her lost legs. *I'll never ride a bike again; never wear a bikini or tight jeans. Nobody will ever love me.*

Bill Bygoves, the minister at Sara's church, had visited her almost every day during her illness. 'Affliction can either be friend or a foe,' he had told her. 'This can either make you bitter or better.' Now Sara turned his words over in her mind. She knew she had to face up to her new life with the same determination and faith that had got her into medical school. *God is with me,* she thought. *Through him I will come out of this a better person.*

Margaret Edwards made it impossible for her daughter to wallow in self-pity. Every morning she breezed into Sara's hospital room and threw open the curtains trumpeting in Welsh, 'Come on! It's a good-to-be-alive morning. Get going!' just as she'd done since Sara was a child.

And there was David. A handsome, soft-spoken third-year medical student, David Webster had been enchanted by Sara's radiant face when she arrived at the university, but he had been too shy to approach her. By chance he had been on call in casualty when Sara was admitted. A committed Christian like Sara, he took responsibility for relaying news of her condition to the students and parishioners praying for her recovery. While she was in a coma he had rarely missed a day at her bedside. Now he plucked up the courage to ask Sara out. As she grew stronger he began 'kidnapping' her from her room, bundling her into a wheelchair, and racing her off down the hospital corridor.

Sara couldn't believe that anyone would ever find her beautiful. But Mary Clewlow changed all that. A fourth-year medical student, Mary had lost a leg to bone cancer. The bubbly girl from Blackpool appeared one day at Sara's bedside, hitched up her fashionable skirt and demanded, 'Which one is my real leg?'

'I can't tell,' Sara said, delightedly. She grilled Mary on how soon she too would have plastic legs, what tights to buy, how to find shoes. After Mary left, Sara thought, *If she's done it, so can I.*

Sara threw herself into daily physiotherapy classes. 'Better not bitter,' became her spiritual theme. First she had to learn to sit up and balance herself, a tricky exercise since the amputation had altered her centre of gravity and she was weak from lying flat for so many months. As she sat on a rubber mat, the physiotherapist would push her to one side over and over again until she could balance herself properly.

On 11 May Sara was ready to try her first steps on artificial legs. As she strapped on the ungainly contraptions she suddenly remembered that just a week before her illness struck she had written in her diary a line from an old Welsh hymn:

'God, I will not walk forward half a step unless you walk beside me.'

Now she repeated those words out loud. Margaret and Dewi held each other tightly as their daughter struggled from her wheelchair and gripped the set of parallel bars. 'Look Mum, I'm walking,' she cried. Slowly she walked the entire 20-foot length of the bars toward them.

The day before, Sara had gone with her parents to a thanksgiving service for her recovery at her local church. David rose to sing in her honour, picked up his guitar, and began: 'One night I dreamed I walked together with my Lord …' but his voice cracked and, overcome with emotion, he couldn't continue.

It was no wonder. The song 'Footprints' tells of a man who looks back at his life and sees two sets of footprints across a beach - his own and God's. During the most discouraging time one set of footprints disappears. The man asks God why he apparently deserted him in his times of trouble. 'During your times of trial and suffering, when you see only one set of footprints in the sand,' God answers, 'it was then that I carried you.'

For the thanksgiving sermon the minister told a story of an old violin that was being auctioned. It was so battered that no one bid for it until an old man came forward, tuned it, and began to play beautiful music. The bidding soared. Anyone or anything can become beautiful in the Master's hands. The sermon was a great inspiration to Sara.

That evening David came to Sara's bedside with a special gift: an old violin that he had bought in a jumble sale years earlier. *Here I am, I weigh only five stones with no legs*, Sara told herself, *and here's a man who thinks I'm beautiful.*

By August, after 20 weeks of painful physiotherapy, Sara was walking on new natural looking legs using walking sticks. In time she vowed she would throw away those sticks.

Just as she was determined to walk unaided Sara never gave up the dream of becoming a doctor. Throughout the months of recovery she had kept an anatomy book by her bed. *Thank God, I haven't lost my hands*, she often thought, *I can still become a gynaecologist or a GP.*

Even Margaret and Dewi doubted whether Sara would be able to return to medical school. The long hours of study taxed able-bodied students: how could Sara ever survive? To add to her difficulties, the powerful medication that kept her alive had impaired her memory of events before her recovery. When she read over her lecture notes it was as if she had never seen them before. If she did return she would have to repeat the entire year.

On 28 April Margaret had wheeled Sara into a histology lecture. Although histology – the science of organic tissues – was her least favourite subject, she felt back where she belonged. But two months later, after her release from hospital, the then dean of the medical school told her bluntly she could not return until she was fully mobile. Taken aback Sara blurted out defiantly, 'No problem. I will learn to drive a specially adapted car'.

Within a week of receiving her new, specially adapted Mini Metro, Sara had passed her driving test. With some misgivings the dean admitted her back to medical school. Helped by her fellow students who carried her books and saved her a front row seat at lectures, she managed well. She zipped round the large Liverpool campus in her car and walked where she could on her artificial legs.

Four years later Sara Edwards graduated as a doctor. Though her medical studies were challenging, the next main event in her life proved to be the greatest challenge of all: walking down the aisle of her parent's village chapel on her fathers arm to the harmony of a Welsh harp. Everyone turned to watch something few thought they would ever see: Sara, a strikingly beautiful bride, walking without sticks up the aisle to meet her future husband David, now Doctor Webster.

Today Sara Webster is still a walking miracle. It was through her continued, determined faith in a faithful God that she found such courage and perseverance. In her home above the living room wall still hangs the old violin. It acts as a constant reminder that anyone who trusts in God can become beautiful 'in the Master's hands!'

Have thine own way, Lord!
Have thine own way!
Thou art the potter:
I am the clay.
Mould me and make me
After thy will,
While I am waiting,
Yielded and still.

Chapter 3

Linked by Prayer

The LORD is near to all who call on him, to all who call on him in truth.
He fulfils the desires of those who fear him; he hears their cry and saves them. Psalm 145:18-19

Faith and prayer can be described as two channels which flow into one and are inseparable. The possibilities of prayer are the possibilities of faith. Prayer and faith are what move the hand of God. They unlock heaven's storehouse of undiminished power from God. They move the hand of the one that moves the world. Prayer is the dominant link between man and God where his healing power is displayed.

We learn a valuable lesson of faith and prayer through the miracle healing of the centurion's servant. The simplicity and strength of the faith of the Roman officer is remarkable, for he believed that it was not necessary for the Lord to go directly to his house in order to have his request granted, 'just say the word,' he said, 'and my servant will be healed' (Matt. 8:8). Jesus praised the man for his faith by saying, 'I have not found anyone in Israel with such great faith'. (v.10). This man's prayer was the expression of his strong faith, and such faith brought forth a prompt answer.

We can learn the same invaluable lesson from the miracle prayer of the Syrophenician woman who went to Jesus on behalf of her stricken daughter. The woman made her daughter's case her own by pleading, 'Lord help me' (Matt. 15:25). It is a wonderful example of intercessory prayer. Jesus seemingly held her off for a while but at last yielded and put his seal of approval upon her by saying: 'O woman, great is your faith. . .' (v. 28).

Today it seems the utmost possibilities of prayer have rarely been realized. The promises of God are so great that it almost staggers our faith and causes us to hesitate with astonishment. His promises to answer, to do and to give 'all things', 'any thing', 'whatsoever', even 'all things whatsoever', are so large, so great, so exceedingly broad, that we stand back in amazement and give ourselves over to questioning and doubt. Let us ever keep in mind, and never for one moment allow ourselves to doubt, the statement that God means what he says and says what he means.

God's promises are his own word. Today, by faith, we can draw on God's healing power, as did the prayer-warriors of the Bible. The Scriptures are filled with precious promises where God invokes his people to pray believing (see Appendix 1).

Robert Diacheysn Jr was one who sought to claim these promises. Answered prayer for him meant the healing of his one-year-old son who had had to endure the sufferings of a neuromuscular disease. Here he journals the events that took place:

Sunday a.m.

'It had been a week of sleepless nights and struggling with our one-year-old son Dakota. As he cried out in pain my wife, Sharon, and I decided to take him to the hospital. He had, at this point, given up the use of his legs.

Sunday p.m.

'After a long day of blood tests, prodding and probing, the doctor decides to admit Dakota for further testing. Diagnosis: unknown.

Monday a.m.

'The doctor informs us that Dakota may have contracted any one of a number of neuromuscular diseases. Some of them considerably more serious than others. We are told he must undergo an EEG, an MRI, and a Spinal tap. We are warned that there is "cause for concern". Diagnosis: still unknown.

Monday p.m.

Upon arriving home, I am greeted with a barrage of phone messages, offering sincere concern and prayers from dear friends. I go on the Internet to send messages to a few friends explaining why I will not be available to fulfil my obligations to them this week. "Coincidentally", I bump into a dear old friend from New Jersey. I tell him the situation and he promises to spread the word to our friends up North, so that they may pray. Suddenly, I remember a close friend here in Florida who has a daily devotional that reaches thousands. I fire off a quick email asking for prayer.

Tuesday noon

Dakota is diagnosed with Guillain-Barre Syndrome: a rare neuromuscular disorder in which the immune system attacks the protein in healthy cells, resulting in temporary paralysis. We are relieved to have a diagnosis and to know that this syndrome is never fatal; it does, however call for constant monitoring of the heart and lungs and can last for weeks, months, or even years!

Tuesday p.m.

Upon arriving home, I am bombarded with phone calls and emails from praying Christians around the world! Everyone seemed to be praying for our baby's healing! I send an update and we return countless local calls asking, "How can we help?" Sharon and Dakota are inundated with hospital visits, gifts, meals, love, and PRAYER, PRAYER, PRAYER!

Wednesday

Dakota's condition takes a dramatic turn – upward! For some reason he is sitting up, kicking his legs, eating, and laughing…coincidence? Or is God sending an "Instant Message" of his own?

Thursday and Friday

Dakota's condition continues to improve remarkably. Our family continues to be blessed by the love and care and constant intercession of God's children everywhere.

Saturday p.m.

Dakota comes home! The Doctor is pleased and amazed at his rapid recovery. He tells us; "He may be completely cured in as little as a week or two!" I go on the computer once more; this time to report the good news. God still hears and answers our prayers! He is a God of miracles!

'Six months have passed since then and Dakota is now completely healed, walking and showing no signs of ever having been infected! We continue to praise the Lord who heals!'

In this age of fast paced, cyberspace technology we can communicate faster than ever before. God can use something like the Internet to carry needs, answers and messages of hope around the globe in just seconds. Yet, he knows the desires of our hearts before the words ever leave our lips. He inhabits the prayers of his people. We can be thankful that we are all 'connected' to a God who never goes 'offline'.

'Before they call I will answer; while they are still speaking I will hear' (Isa. 65:24).

Another method of prayer is through the biblically prescribed means of the anointing service, as described by James:

> Is any one of you sick? He should call the elders of the church to pray over him and anoint him with oil in the name of the Lord. And the prayer offered in faith will make the sick person well; the Lord will raise him up (James 5:14-16).

Pastor Ken Clothier shares how an anointing service for one of his parishioners in York brought results that baffled even the medical staff.

'On one of my home visits I was puzzled to find Charles Barker sitting on a chair with his trousers rolled up his legs. His feet rested in a bowl of warm water, and his legs appeared very swollen. I quickly discovered that he had gangrene and was trying to encourage the circulation of the blood to his lower limbs. His condition worsened over the next few weeks and he was admitted into hospital.

'The nurse in charge of his ward brought him the fearful news that he would need to have at least one of his legs amputated. With his customary smiling face he turned to the nurse and said, "No…that will not be necessary." Here is a qualified nurse, in cooperation with the doctor, understanding the gravity of the situation and presenting to her patient the only life-saving cure she knows, and the patient replies by saying "No, that will not be necessary"!

'Charles invited the elder of the Church and me to the hospital to conduct a service of anointing. The expression on the nurse's face when we arrived will live with me forever. She looked at us as though we belonged to another planet. It soon became obvious that our beloved brother had made all the necessary arrangements for our arrival. When I asked the nurse if we could use a private room for anointing, she simply looked at us, incredulously pointing in the direction of an empty room and appearing utterly speechless.

'This was an awesome moment which needed tremendous faith and I felt totally unworthy to lead in the service that was to follow. The realization struck me forcefully that if any of us were harbouring a single sin, however small, then God would not be able to help us. We searched our hearts. We read. We prayed. The anointing followed, but nothing of a miraculous nature took place. After a while the elder and I left the hospital and made our way home.

'A short time later Charles was discharged from hospital. The wonderful news is that although there was no apparent instant and complete cure, the blood circulation in his legs gradually began to return back to normal. He was back on his bike spreading the gospel literature through the villagers where he lived, just as he had been accustomed to doing before for many years. One year later our Charles Barker returned to the hospital for a check-up. A new doctor read his notes and said, "Mr Barker, if I had been here a year ago, I would have certainly removed your leg." Does God answer prayer?'

'You will pray to him, and he will hear you' (Job 22:27).

Brendalyn Martin received healing from diabetes as a result of personal, persevering prayer. She was diagnosed with diabetes and hospitalized with a blood sugar of 1293 on May 24 1999. She was severely dehydrated and the doctors and nurses in the Intensive Care Unit had said that with a blood sugar level that high she ought to have been in a coma or even dead. However Brendalyn knew that through all this God's hands were upon her. She continues,

'Before I was hospitalized, when I knew something was wrong but did not know what, I continually prayed and stood on God's Word that "by his stripes we are healed". After being in hospital for a week I was released with my blood sugars still at the 200 mark and taking 74 units of insulin a day. I continued to pray that I would not need the insulin, especially since I have a deep aversion to needles. Within a week it was down to 100 and I had problems keeping it up. Over the next three weeks, they lowered the doses and a month after leaving the hospital I was taken off insulin and placed on one Glyburide tablet a day, the lowest dose.

'I continued to pray that I would not need any medications at all and testified to almost everyone I met of how God had kept me in the palm of his hand and was healing my body. Three weeks later I was taken off the Glyburide, since my blood sugars continued to drop too low. My doctor said she had never seen anyone's blood sugar drop at such a dramatic rate and come completely off all medications in such a short period of time. She agreed with me in prayer that God continues to heal me.

'I continued to praise the Lord and keep myself covered in prayer. Two months after being in such a critical state that I should have died, I was no longer on any medication.'

Today Brendalyn continues to prosper and gives all the glory to God for maintaining her. With his guidance she keeps her blood sugars under control with diet and exercise only. She concludes, 'I know that my prayers and those of my family and friends are the reason I am alive and well today.'

'The Lord is near to all who call on him, to all who call on him in truth. He fulfils the desires of those who fear him; he hears their cry and saves them' (Ps. 145:18-19).

Chapter 4

Hope Again

'For I know the plans I have for you,' declares the Lord, 'plans to prosper you and not to harm you, plans to give you hope and a future.' Jeremiah 29:11-12

The sick man was lying on his mat and occasionally lifting his head to gaze at the pool. Suddenly a compassionate face bent over him and the words, 'Do you want to get well?' arrested his attention (Jn. 5:6). Hope came to his heart. He felt in some way he was to have help. But the glow of encouragement soon faded. He remembered how often he had tried to reach the pool and now he had little prospect of living till it should be stirred. He turned away wearily saying 'Sir, I have no one to help me into the pool when the water is stirred. While I am trying to get in, someone else goes down ahead of me' (v.7).

Jesus bids him, 'Get up! Pick up your mat and walk' (v.7). With a new hope the sick man looks at Jesus. The cripple's faith now takes hold of Jesus. Without question he obeys and as he does so his whole body responds. Every nerve and muscle thrills with new life and healthful action comes to his once-crippled limbs. Acting on a renewed hope in the word of Christ, he was made whole.

Gary Zarback discovered the miraculous effect of rekindling such a renewed hope in Christ. In 1998 Gary was diagnosed with terminal nasopharnyx cancer, an invasive brain tumour of terrible malignancy. He described himself as one without hope, a former Buddhist dropout, devoid of faith in God and, at 117 lbs., deteriorating in health. He confessed that the only thing he still possessed was a terrifying fear of dying, and the strong steady love of his wife and sons.

'In my fifty-nine years of life, I'd been many things: a father of six children, a musician, a long-time drug addict and hustler; living my life in the fast lane and a confirmed agnostic. So, here I was at the end of my life – so soon! I was full of love, but still spiritually barren and crying my heart out. But you know what happened? Yes, the Lord made himself known to me and Jesus Christ came into my life, at last! I, Gary Z. was born again!

'I was totally bedridden, barely alive, my mortal nutrition flowing through tubes in my body. I had lost the swallow reflex several months ago, so I had been unable to consume normal food, but spiritual nutrition was flowing into my body from all directions! People I've never met or seen were praying for me in a little Church across the state, thanks to one of my loving sisters-in-law!

'Although I couldn't leave my bed, hooked to a morphine pump twenty-four hours a day to relieve the constant agony of the hungry tumour in my head, my heart began filling with hope. Hope! – something that had become foreign to me. I was going deaf, losing my vision and preparing to die, but now that God was in my life, I was no longer terrified of dying. With my hand in the Lord's, I was ready to die with dignity and in peace.

'New strength began pouring into me. With help I became able to leave my bed and walk a bit every day, and I began regaining my lost weight: 117, 120,122 lbs. I began attending my small neighbourhood church for the very first time in my life. I regained 125, then 128 lbs. My swallow reflex began working again and I was able to taste my first honest-to-goodness food in over seven months. I reached 135, 140, 145 lbs., and eventually began riding a mountain bike, a few blocks a day at first, increasing to twenty miles every day. Still the weight kept pouring on to my once ravaged and wasted body. By the time July 1998 rolled around which was the month I should have died, my weight was at 160 lbs. and I was able to play my beloved music again. This time it was in church with my eighteen-year-old son David.

'And still my weight increased, to 165, 175, and then 190 lbs. My doctor, a top specialist in the field of oncology, was amazed, having not seen me since his diagnosis nine months previously. Eighty wonderful pounds of healthy, living flesh had miraculously rejoined my once doomed and dying body. I prayed and praised and gave still more prayer and thanks! I got baptized in a loving church, attended several revivals, and brought some old friends from the other side of the tracks to God and to church.

'And before I knew it, I was celebrating my sixtieth birthday. Praise the Lord! The feeding tube has been removed and at present, I'm eating normally again. I'm nearly totally off the morphine and other drugs I was once so dependant on to save my life from misery, and it is now almost certain that the brain tumour inside my head is now dead. It is no longer destroying the wonderful body God had provided for me. It is no longer the root of all my fears and uncertainties. It is now just a hidden, ugly scarred mass of inert tissue residing in my head, unnoticed, but never to be forgotten by me or my friends and family.

'I have much more than my life back: I also have The Lord in my life, and the knowledge of the price Jesus paid for me and you to be free. I truly have a hope again. Praise God!'

Gary's story is a wonderful testimony of how hope in the Almighty God has the power to provide a resurgence of healing. The Psalmist David said 'Happy is he who has the God of Jacob for his help, whose hope is in the Lord' (Ps.146:5 NKJV). Gary's experience reveals the assurance that God is just as willing to restore the sick now as when the Holy Spirit spoke these words through the psalmist. In God there is a healing balm for every disease, restoring power for every infirmity. His desire for every human being is expressed in the words: 'Beloved, I wish above all things that you may prosper and be in health, even as your soul prospers' (3 Jn. 2 NKJV).

Andrea Tawney also shared that desire. She was diagnosed with an illness called Systemic Erythematosus Lupus: a long-term debilitation involving joints, skin, and potentially all major organs. Andrea tells her dramatic healing story:

'It was the early fall of 1981. I was just a month into my first classroom teaching job in our brand new Christian school. I had the split third/fourth grade and a teaching partner. I usually taught Sunday school, Vacation Bible school, youth groups, at camps and in women's classes. Christian day school was an exciting new venture.

'The lupus symptoms started simply enough. I was supervising students during lunch break and an out of control basketball came my way. It knocked into the back of my right hand, jarring it. It stung, but was too minor to pay attention to. The next day my hand was stiff. A week later the joints in my fingers were still painful, and within just a couple of weeks my elbow, hip, and knee on the right side were sore. No amount of aspirin stopped the discomfort so it was time to have the doctor check it out.

'He tested for rheumatoid arthritis but that showed negative. So he sent me to a specialist. This doctor did extensive tests and finally diagnosed lupus. It was a tentative diagnosis, since this seemed to be a rather vague sort of disease. The typical analgesic type arthritis medications were prescribed, but, aside from causing stomach upset, had little effect. The joint pain increased, and the medications were adjusted. As the medications got stronger, the stomach pain got stronger and the joint pain grew worse.

'As soon as the diagnosis of lupus was made, my husband and I asked for prayer from our church, friends not affiliated to our church, and family in the United States and Canada. Both my husband and I had been Christians since our teens, and we were fully confident that it was within God's ability to heal me. Whether or not, in his sovereignty, he would, we didn't know, but we would trust him for the best for our family.

'As the weeks went by, the pain increased. Many people prayed for me, laid hands on me, anointed me with oil, and encouraged me constantly. The pain became so severe I could no longer clap during worship. It hurt to hold a pen or lift a book – which for a teacher is a disaster. We bought a compact style of Bible because I could not carry or even hold my study version. I used both hands to pick up bottles, cups or items of any weight. It hurt to walk, sit or stand. Even the weight of the sheet on my feet at night was painful.

'While to my friends and family the Lord seemed to be speaking of healing and encouragement; to me He said, "Yea, though I walk through the valley of the shadow of death, I will fear no evil; for you are with me; your rod and your staff, they comfort me" (Ps. 23:4 NKJV). I didn't find that so very encouraging, but I knew I could trust him. My husband and I were both sure that with such rapid development of the disease, if God didn't heal me, I would soon be in serious trouble. In the world's understanding, my prognosis was not good.

'During the following autumn, I attended a seminar on healing with a number of friends.

They were filled with the highest hopes for my healing. I was not experiencing hopefulness; I was probably more resigned. Pain and coping seemed to fill my time and take up all my energy. I knew God would do what he would do, and that was enough for me. At the seminar God dealt with me powerfully in the area of forgiveness. We saw miracles of physical healing that day, but none of them were for me. My healing was emotional and spiritual and while it was a wonderfully exciting day, I was still in pain.

'The holidays came and went, the pain came and stayed, and I grew more and more fatigued. In the New Year our church planned a seminar on worship. A powerful worship leader came to teach. The Friday night seminar was excellent, and during the ministry time, I received prayer. While God spoke to my heart, there was nothing from him for my body.

'On the Saturday night, during the ministry time again, I received prayer. This time the Holy Spirit overwhelmed me physically. I could barely stand; my body felt heavily limp. I couldn't move and was hardly able to breathe. I could feel my body being drained of something, with powerful waves flowing down from my head to my feet. I knew without a doubt that the lupus was leaving me, and a tremendous relief filled me. I didn't say much; I couldn't say much!

'The next day in church I could clap during worship with the best of the clappers and everyone rejoiced with me. I returned to the doctor and as he checked each of my joints, there was no pain. I was able to grip his hand strongly, when prior to this, I could not grip at all. I told him that God had healed me through the prayers of my Christian friends, and all he could say was "Well, tell your friends they did you good!" I never returned to the doctor.

'I remembered the words God had spoken to me about the valley of the shadow of death, and I realized that I focused on being in the valley. I didn't see that the valley was filled with shadows, nothing real, and that the promise was that I would pass through. My faith in God's ability and desire to heal me never wavered; my faith that he would heal me wobbled constantly. I could only cling to his love, and the sure knowledge that, in his sovereignty, he would do what was best for my family and me.'

Because of the steadfast prayers from everyone around Andrea, her eyes were fixed on the Lord and on his faithfulness. It is not what he does for and with us, but that he is. Just knowing this is enough. He hears us and chooses in his almighty wisdom, generously mixed with love and grace, what is best for us. Our challenge is to hope on, even when our surroundings seem dark or dismal. The Scriptures assure us, 'Call on to me and I will answer you and show you great and mighty things which you don't know about' (Jer. 33:3 NKJV).

Veronica Neybert found herself spirituality challenged one day when she received an unexpected call from her doctor. There was a sense of urgency in his voice as he reported that the mammogram had come back questionable. The doctor wanted to schedule an appointment with the radiologist for a biopsy to determine if the spots on the mammograms were cancerous.

Slowly the thought that she might have cancer began to sink in. The challenge to Veronica's faith became more daunting as she realized that cancer was something that had run through her family. Her sister had died at the age of forty from cancer. Her father, grandmother, and other members of her family, had had various kinds of cancer. It was rampant in the family on both her father's and mother's sides. Her mother had had a lumpectomy for a cancerous breast tumour. Amid all these revolving thoughts she knew above all that this was not a time to panic and think of what might happen; it was a time to pray.

'I shared my problem with a few trusted friends. It was decided to have an evening of special prayer, laying on of hands and asking for God's mercy and healing touch. We spent time in praise and worship. After confessing our sins and receiving his forgiveness, we laid our petitions before Jesus. I was anointed with blessed oil and stood on God's word in Exodus 23:25; 'Worship the Lord your God, and his blessing will be on your food and water. I will take away sickness from among you'. I reminded the Lord that 'by his stripes we were healed' and that 'with him all things were possible'. During the prayer time a deep sense of peace and warmth covered my body. I knew in my heart that everything would be all right. I still had to walk in faith and see how Jesus was going to deal with the cancer.

'I visited the surgeon's office and had my pre-operation physical and all the necessary blood work done for the surgical procedure. The following week I went back for my final check-up before surgery with the surgeon. Before leaving his office I asked him if I could pray with him. He said, "Yes, I'm a Christian." I told him I would not consent to surgery unless I first prayed over him and asked God to guide him and give him the necessary wisdom to make the correct choices for my medical condition. After a moment of prayer, he thanked me and said that he really appreciated my praying with him. It was the first time he had ever had a patient pray with him.

'Two days later I was on the wheelchair waiting for surgery. "When are you going to act God? Or are they going to find the tumours are benign? I really don't want to go through the biopsies and the pain etc. Let your will be done Lord." A nurse came to get me. She wheeled me into the x-ray room instead of surgery because they needed to do another mammogram. I saw my old mammograms with the little spots circled on the wall in front of me. I dragged myself with all my tubes and went through the procedures again. The technician asked me to sit on the chair and wait until they examined this set of mammograms. I told her not to worry; I couldn't go too far dragging my tubes, barefoot and dressed in a gown split open down the back!

'I was beginning to feel giddy by this time. I prayed and asked our Lord how and when he would honour his word. "I just don't want to go through surgery", I kept saying to the Lord. After a long wait, the technician returned with the radiologist. "I am recommending that surgery be cancelled." I threw up my arms and yelled, "Thank you Jesus! Praise your holy name! Thank you!" The radiologist looked at me as if I'd lost my mind. The technician appeared to be angry but the cute little LPN gave me the high sign and had a grin from ear to ear. As I went down the hall back to the holding area, I yelled, "Jesus healed me!" The surgeon came in and said that he would have to check the new mammogram and talk to the radiologist. After looking at them, he agreed that there was no need for surgery.

'I went home and after sharing the news with my brother-in-law, who is a doctor, I found out that they just don't do last minute repeat mammograms before surgery. It was divine intervention. God's ways certainly are not my ways but thank God, he is looking after me and guiding me as I walk the path he has laid out for me. I can do all things when Jesus Christ is my strength.'

Today, six years on, Veronica has no recurrence of cysts or tumours in her breasts. Her annual mammograms have all been normal and she continues to experience a fulfilled hope in the God of all Hope.

'We wait in hope for the Lord; he is our help and our shield. In him our hearts rejoice, for we trust in his holy name. May your unfailing love rest upon us, O Lord, even as we put our hope in you'
(Ps 33:20-22).

Chapter 5

A Renewed Journey

I will lead the blind by ways they have not known, along unfamiliar paths I will guide them; I will turn the darkness into light before them and make the rough places smooth. These are the things I will do; I will not forsake them.
Isaiah 42:16

It must have been humbling being told that to be healed you must wash seven times in a dirty river. Yet this was the experience of Naaman, the Syrian captain (2 Kgs. 5:1-14). The Scriptures describe him as a 'great man', a 'valiant soldier', and 'highly regarded'. In order to be healed of his leprosy this mighty soldier would have to subject himself to the miry waters of the river Jordan, according to instructions which, though given by Elisha, were relayed to Naaman by a messenger. 'Surely,' Naaman thought, 'this man of God could at least see me himself! and stand and call on the name of the Lord his God, wave his hand over the spot and cure me of my leprosy?' (2 Kgs. 5:11.)

When we think of healing we often imagine an instantaneous occurrence. Although there are experiences where this happens, oftentimes a period of healing may involve making an unmapped journey during which only God knows the ultimate destination – a journey where lessons such as trust, humility, faith and forgiveness are learnt. You could imagine that after washing three times and seeing no improvement, Naaman was ready to give up. How humiliated he must have felt! After the sixth wash there was still no change – the shame and embarrassment must have been unbearable. It's in times like these that the challenge is to 'let go and let God'. The Psalmist captures this challenge when he says, 'Be still and know that I am God' (Ps. 46:10). God was leading Naaman on a journey of healing upon which he was to learn to be still in the presence of God, to experience humility and to trust in God.

The seventh wash, and the Scriptures declare, 'his flesh was restored and became clean like that of a young boy' (2 Kgs. 5:14). There is need of much patience on the journey of healing.

Carolyn Scheidies is one who embarked upon such a patient journey. It was 30 years before she returned to her school where the tragic events that led to her debilitating disease took place. Carolyn had been asked to return to her High School as the guest speaker at a special anniversary reunion service. She recalls her journey:

'I marvelled that I was there at all. I'd returned walking. Of all people, I'd been asked to speak. I'd returned the author of 11 books with hundreds of other published credits. I'd returned a success and they all rejoiced with me. They rejoiced because 30 years ago when they knew me, I had been confined to a wheelchair.

'It began one January, after a serious bout of Strep Throat and just before my thirteenth birthday. I began to feel as though I'd been run over by a truck. I hurt all over. My arms and legs didn't want to move. To say I was scared would be too mild. By the time school ended that spring, everyone knew something was wrong. I was active. I loved to run and play. I loved being outdoors. I was a tomboy. Suddenly I found excuses to stay indoors, found reasons not to participate in activities which caused me pain. I tried to hide all the pain and terror, but I failed. Even the other students, my friends, realized something was wrong.

'Concerned, my parents took me to the doctor. After a battery of tests the results came back – Juvenile Rheumatoid Arthritis. So began a long journey for me. Within a year I was in a wheelchair despite every effort to keep my legs straight. My parents took me from doctor to doctor, from one rehabilitation centre to another, where I got various degrees of help. I always battled pain and depression and the belief that I wasn't of use to anyone. I felt I was a burden to everyone.

'During that time, there where many caring people who prayed for me. However there were also many unanswered questions in my mind. Why didn't God answer in the way I wanted him to? Why wasn't he listening? I'd ask my father. He just told me to trust God. But I knew my parents were hurting as much as I was.

'At night when all was still, when an owl hooted outside my window, when a lone coyote howled in the distance, when sleep evaded me, more and more I'd play with ideas and words and couplets until a poem or song took shape in my mind. Over and over I'd try to impale it in my mind. With my legs and hands encased in splints, I was helpless to write my creations on paper. What I did have were very understanding parents. "Mum! Dad!" I'd call in the dead of night. One or the other would stumble into the room, sit down, and pick up paper and pen and write down my poem, or song. The next morning there it was, a creation born out of my own deep hurts, my searching, my pain. Little did I realize that my illness released me to write reams of poems and songs and other things which spoke to my situation. It honed my writing skills and ignited my desire to write as a career. I also began to learn God was more than the sum of my wants.

'Though I didn't realize it, God wasn't finished with me yet. A few years later, my father drove me hundreds of miles to a conference where he knew they prayed for the sick. On the way we broke the trip into two days because I couldn't handle travelling for long periods of time. The services were uplifting. I felt encouraged, but sceptical. After all, I was used to all sorts of individuals and ministers praying for me. Sometimes I felt I was their latest challenge. However this time something was different. The last day when Dad took me up to the front the minister looked at me and said, "I've been fasting and praying for you this week." As I stared at him, he placed his hand gently on my head and began to pray.

'I felt as though a hundred locks had suddenly opened. The pain disappeared. God healed me of the active disease. My legs didn't straighten. My hands didn't look any less gnarled, but at that moment I began to improve.

'Back at the motel Dad tried to get me to take my painkillers, but I refused. "I don't need them," I told him. And I didn't. For the first time in a long time, I spent a peaceful, restful night. The next morning we started home. What a difference! Instead of lying in the back seat gritting my teeth, I sat up and enjoyed the passing scenery. Instead of waiting for the trip to end, I said, "Let's keep going. I'm doing fine." And I was...we drove all the way home without staying over.

'In the next months and years, I learned to dress myself and pretty much take care of my personal needs. But I was still tied to the wheelchair, a wheelchair I was not strong enough to wheel myself. Different rehabilitation centres suggested a variety of treatments, which did little to straighten my legs. Surgery was hesitantly suggested, but there were no guarantees that any surgery techniques available at the time would have lasting benefits. They did suggest straightening my legs, but then they wouldn't bend. That would bring on a whole new set of problems. The answer was no.

'When we moved to Iowa, Margaret Freeman, an author from our church, took me under her wing. She helped me sell my first story and my publishing career began. By this time I'd set my sights on a journalism degree.

'The college I attended wasn't accessible by today's standards, but it was good for me at the time. Whilst I was there I met Dr Ellis who wanted to help me. Joint replacements had just hit the medical establishment. The problem was that they were only guaranteed for seven to ten years. That's why their use at the time was confined to the elderly. I was in my early twenties – joint replacement surgery might get me up and walking, but it would also almost guarantee I'd need surgery again in the future.

'Dr Ellis went out of his way to secure funding for the massive reconstructive surgery involved in helping me get back on my feet. He even took my x-rays to the founder of the then new procedure for total joint replacement to make sure he'd do the very best for me. I was hesitant, scared. What if I couldn't do all the things I could already do? What if this procedure made things worse for me? What if? Patiently Dr Ellis answered my questions. He loved the Lord and he cared about what happened to me. He advised the surgery. My own prayers led me to the same conclusion. Finally, the summer after I graduated from college, I checked into the hospital. I had visions of gracefully walking out of the hospital, smiling at all those who looked down on the "poor girl in the wheelchair".

'More than anything, what Dr Ellis gave me was hope. What I did not envision, were the weeks of surgery – different surgeries, reconstructive surgeries – required to allow the new joints to work. Not even Dr Ellis realized until he got started what it would take to get me back on my feet. I did not envisage weeks and months of healing and pain and relearning how to walk with full-length leg braces and crutches.

I did not envisage all the determination I would need to stay the course. I also did not envisage the wonderful friends who helped along the way, who prayed with me and for me, who encouraged and supported me – including one special person.

'One year after my surgery, I walked down the aisle of our little church without crutches, without braces, to take the hand of the man who became my husband – a man who accepted me just the way I was. Yes, the years brought more surgeries: another set of knees, four hip replacements, and two ankle fusions, but they also brought two beautiful children by caesarean.

'The young girl who looked on herself as a burden, now 30 years later stood in front of the congregation at my school as the guest speaker. What she saw – what I saw – was a good God who works through my failures and my pain to give me a platform to reach out to other hurting people. What I know is that God is in control, and I'm glad I belong to him.'

'But they that wait upon the Lord shall renew their strength; they shall mount up with wings as eagles; they shall run, and not be weary; and they shall walk, and not faint' (Isa. 40:31 KJV).

Eva Eveson also embarked on a journey of a different kind. At four months pregnant she wondered if she would ever be able to behold her miracle child.

'"Ahhhh!" I screamed as I raised my hands to cover my face and slammed on the brakes. A blinding hot flame shot through my eyes. "God, help me", I prayed silently. Tears began to course down my cheeks and I was only able to open my eyes just enough to focus on the road ahead. The drive home was a nightmare. I immediately removed my contact lens. I hadn't worn glasses in years, I didn't even own a spare pair but I figured if I rested my eyes a bit, I'd be okay. I was wrong.

'For the next several weeks I kept silent as the recurring pain came upon me each time I went into the sunshine. By the first month of the year I wore sunglasses all day, even inside my home. I don't know why I was afraid to tell someone that I was having this problem. Perhaps I thought the sensitivity to light was a part of my pregnancy.

'One day my eyes began to pour thick mucus. Then I noticed that having to wear my sunglasses went way into the evening. At night the light from the television was too much for me. One afternoon, I pulled a blanket over my head and cried. It was time to admit that this was not normal and to say something to my husband.

'The following day he drove me to an ophthalmologist's office where I was given a diagnosis I have yet to remember. It was three very long words – that I remember! The doctor tried to sound optimistic, but his words left me shaking.

'"I'm going to dilate your eyes," he began, "then I will put a patch on your right eye. That's the one I'm most concerned about. I want you to put these drops in both eyes three times a day, and keep this eyepatch on unless you are sleeping."

'"Am I going to lose my vision?" I asked.

'"I'm not as concerned about your left eye as I am your right", he said, avoiding the question. "I only wish you had come in sooner."

'At this point I should have been well acquainted with God and his healing power and miraculous handiwork. The very fact that I was presently four months pregnant was a miracle. The previous September, after months of gynaecological difficulties, I had undergone exploratory surgery to determine exactly what my problem was. By this point in my life I had conceived three times but never made it to the second trimester. My doctors told me that I had endometriosis. They told me, "Your uterus is in such a state as to make it nearly impossible to get pregnant much less carry to term." I had two stepchildren whom I loved dearly, but I wanted one of my own! My mother, who stood behind me, gently placed her hand on my shoulder and said, "Where's your faith?" I nodded. "God," I prayed, "if you want me to get pregnant, then make me pregnant. If you don't, then give me the understanding of your will." Six days later, I conceived.

'This small wonder was growing inside me, but now my new fear was that I would now not be able to see the baby I had so longed for. After the doctor had examined my eyes I spent the next three weeks in blind confusion. I couldn't see well enough to read. I couldn't study my Bible. The days seemed to drag on forever.

'Somewhere in this three-week interim, my mother came for a visit. She repeated the same words she had spoken a few months before. "Where is your faith?" I honestly couldn't answer that. With God's recent move in my life, one would think that I would have just said, "Oh, but of course! Okay, God. Heal me!" But the pain was so real and the situation seemed somehow bigger than him. This time I would have to rely on the faith of my mother. Mother and I prayed together. Within three weeks, my eyes were back to normal. I had not lost any vision in either eye! However, the doctor insisted that I stay out of contact lenses for a while and wear glasses exclusively. I wasn't happy, my vanity being what it was, but I agreed.

'In June, 1981 a beautiful baby girl with soft, blond hair and large, blue eyes was born just forty minutes into her due date. It was nine months to the day since I had been told that pregnancy and delivery would be impossible. For nine months I secretly prayed for a little girl with blond hair and blue eyes. God had given me the desire of my heart and the eyes with which to see her.

'That year the problem with my eyes reoccurred. The diagnosis was the same. The prognosis was as dim as it had been the first time. But this time, my attitude about faith and healing were different. "I want to see you in a week", the doctor told me. Ironically, my mother was due for a visit that day. As soon as she walked in the door, I told her about my doctor's visit. "There's a prayer session tonight at the church", I told her. "I can go and have the elders, deacons, and prayer-warriors anoint me and pray for me. Do you want to come with me?"

'"Absolutely!" Mother exclaimed positively.

'The following week I marched into the doctor's office, jumped into the chair, and exclaimed, "You won't find anything wrong with these eyes, Dr Sanders. These eyes are perfectly healed."

'"I don't think so", Dr. Sanders said from across the room. He switched the light off and walked toward me. "I'm not expecting a complete healing for several weeks. But hopefully most of the blisters are gone."

'"You don't understand," I told him, "there will be no blisters because I gave this over to God and he has healed me once and for all!"

'Dr Sanders pointed the light of his ophthalmoscope toward me. "Uh-huh. We'll see about....Huh? My goodness..!"

'I grinned. "They're gone, aren't they?"

'"They sure are", he said, sounding rather surprised.

'"Told you", I said, still grinning.

'"Well, I don't know that I believe in the God thing..." he reverted, as he sat back down at his desk.

'"Well, I do," I responded full of assurity, "and right now, that's all that really matters, isn't it?"'

Eva's journey was one that led her to a renewed strength in God. Today she is the author of a number of books and through her established ministry of intercessory prayer has become a channel of strength in encouraging others on their spiritual journey.

**'But for you who revere my name, the sun of righteousness will rise with healing in its wings'
(Mal. 4:2).**

Betty Huff's most dramatic healing through prayer occurred in 1954 after the birth of her second daughter, Kathleen. Her pregnancy at the age of twenty-one was normal until her waters broke six weeks early. Instead of a normal labour, the placenta began to break apart (placenta abruption) and an emergency C-section was performed. That was the beginning of her nightmarish ordeal. She recalls that only the fervent prayers from many different denominations saved her and the baby. (Kathleen is now a grandmother of four.)

'After the delivery the doctor told my husband that he had lost the baby and only gave me a fifty-fifty chance to live. Later, the baby began to breathe on her own, but my life hung in the balance for the next three months. Six weeks after the birth I had a massive post-partum haemorrhage with blood pouring from every orifice in the body. Six orderlies ran to the operating room, each holding an IV of whole blood flowing into my unconscious body. A hysterectomy was performed vaginally and the problem seemed to be solved. Two weeks later another massive haemorrhage tore out all the stitches and I was given only oxygen during the mop-up and repair, for fear that in my weakened state an anaesthetic might kill me.

'At this point my Christian doctor began some serious research coupled with prayer. Also praying were my Catholic family, my

Jewish in-laws, our Baptist landlords and our Seventh Day Adventist neighbours.

'Another two weeks, another haemorrhage. My doctor flew from California to Chicago and found good news and bad news. The bad news was there had only been three cases like mine in the prior ten-year period and all three women had died. The good news was they knew it was caused by a lack of fibrogen (blood clotting agent) in the blood. The lack of fibrogen was caused by not eating enough protein. (My only source of dietary protein had been an occasional peanut butter sandwich and a glass of milk.)

'My doctor flew home with a tiny vial of protein-enriched plasma. My final haemorrhage occurred that evening and the life-giving vial was attached to the catheter in my arm. I came out of my comatose state the next morning. The room was flooded with sunshine, the birds were chirping and my mother was singing "Happy Birthday to You!" I was twenty-two that day!'

Sometimes the journey of healing in itself can be a painful one. It may involve much despair and emotional scarring on the way. During such times, when we look at the example of Christ, who ultimately took upon himself our personal journey of life and lived a life which was ours, we can live a life which is his. Isaiah reminds us of the path he trod before us:

He was despised and rejected by men, a man of sorrows, and familiar with suffering. Like one from whom men hide their faces he was despised, and we esteemed him not.

Surely he took up our infirmities and carried our sorrows, yet we considered him stricken by God, smitten by him, and afflicted. But he was pierced for our transgressions, he was crushed for our iniquities; the punishment that brought us peace was upon him, and by his wounds we are healed.

We all, like sheep, have gone astray, each of us has turned to his own way; and the Lord has laid on him the iniquity of us all.

He was oppressed and afflicted, yet he did not open his mouth; he was led like a lamb to the slaughter, and as a sheep before her shearers is silent, so he did not open his mouth.

By oppression and judgment he was taken away. And who can speak of his descendants? For he was cut off from the land of the living; for the transgression of my people he was stricken (Isa. 53:3-9).

Chapter 6

I Do a New Thing

See, I am doing a new thing! Now it springs up;
do you not perceive it?
I am making a way in the desert and streams in
the wasteland. Isaiah 43:19

Imagine what it must have been like for Hannah. Here was a woman who desperately wanted a child of her own. With each passing year the possibilities seemed more and more futile. Others constantly provoked her barrenness and, despite the love of her husband, the Scriptures portrayed a woman who experienced much grief and 'bitterness of soul' who 'wept much', and was of a 'sorrowful spirit' (1 Sam. 1:10,15).

At a time when Hannah could have allowed such discouragement to abandon her faith, the Scriptures reveal how, in the midst of her mental anguish, she turned to God in prayer. 'O

Lord Almighty, if you will only look upon your servant's misery and remember me, and not forget your servant but give her a son, then I will give him to the Lord for all the days of his life, and no razor will ever be used on his head' (1 Sam. 1:11). Her prayer was answered. 'I prayed for this child, and the Lord has granted me what I asked of him' (1 Sam. 1:27). The Lord was able to 'do a new thing' for Hannah and make what was initially a barren experience become 'a way in the desert and streams in the wasteland'.

One of the blessed assurances for a Christian is to know that whatever circumstances we find ourselves in in life, with God, 'all things are possible'. To know this is a great comfort. 'God's ways are not our ways neither his thoughts our thoughts'. God in his infinite wisdom knows in every given situation what is best for us. Whatever may come our way, God is in control.

This was a lesson which David and Sherene Harper were to learn. I first met them whilst pastoring at a Church in Trowbridge in England. They were both keen and active members. They had been married for four years and in that time had been trying for a baby. During my pastorate with them, I encountered their dejection and discouragement when it seemed all attempts for a child failed. They share their story:

'The wonders of God became a reality in my life when I met David in Jamaica, the home of my birth, in 1990. Whilst he was on holiday we fell in love and got married in 1993. We set up our home in England.

'We started to try for a family a year after we got married. With no success we went to see our doctor. From there we were sent to see a specialist. We had some tests taken and the results showed I had a blocked tube. We would never be able to have children naturally. I was told I would need an operation to clear the tube.

'After the operation in 1997, we were told that the tube was badly damaged. Added to this there was only a ten per cent chance of me conceiving. If it didn't happen in the first year of the operation my chances would be nil. Our only choice would be IVF where my chance to conceive naturally would be one in a million.

'It was very hard for me to accept. I cried every day. I felt ashamed of myself and at the thought of letting David down. I wouldn't talk about the problem. I didn't let my family know. I was so depressed I even tried to take my life on two occasions. I tried to push David away from me. I told him to go and find someone who could give him children. His parents told him to leave me, because a married couple ought to have children. His answer to me all the time was that he married me because he loved me, not because I would give him children.

'David and I grew closer. He was there more for me than I was there for him. I sometimes told him it was my problem, but he always said it was our problem. I forgot sometimes that he was just as hurt as me.

'We had our first attempt at IVF in 1998. It didn't work. We tried again in 1999; again it was a failure. We had spent more than £7,500 on IVF, not including time off work without pay.

'During that time I didn't know who I was or what I believed in. I lost touch with the Lord. After prayer I would get up off my knees, feeling the same way as when I went down – with an oppressed heart.

'It was when we decided to go for adoption that I started to accept that I would never be able to give birth to a child. One day I was talking about adoption at work saying that my heart was not one hundred per cent with it, because I wanted to give birth to a child of my own. One of my work mates said, "It's not a egg from you and a sperm from your partner that will make you good parents, it's the love you show and give to a child." I thought about what she said and my heart was more inclined toward adoption.

'I read 1 Samuel 1: 1-28 and 1 Samuel 2: 1-2. I felt how Hannah was feeling when she was praying to the Lord. That night I got up from my knees in prayer feeling a different person; it was as if a burden had been lifted from me.

From that night I didn't feel bitter any more when I saw children in the streets or when people talked about their children. If David told me that he loved me I believed him. The only thing was that I still didn't feel a woman, and when I looked in the mirror I still saw an ugly person.

'We were accepted for the adoption. We booked a holiday for three weeks in Jamaica and we were going to tell our family about the problems we were having, together with the decision to adopt a child.

'Two weeks before our holiday David kept telling me that I was pregnant. I had stopped taking notice of when my periods were due and I took no notice of what David was saying. He kept asking me to take a home pregnancy test. Finally I took the test and in my anger threw it at him. I didn't even look at the results. I heard David crying and saying, "Yes, thank you God." I didn't believe the results. I took four more tests. All were positive. That night I didn't sleep. I prayed, giving thanks to the Lord.

'I had a wonderful nine months of pregnancy. I went into labour one week early. During this time, the baby's heartbeat dropped from 171 to 50 beats. The doctor was worried about the heartbeat and he called in four more doctors to check. We told them that the baby would be fine because this baby is a miracle baby, the Lord has given us this baby and nothing is going to be wrong.

'I gave birth to a healthy baby girl. We called her Shania Alisha Sherene Harper. After six years of trying to have a child, the Lord had answered our prayers.

'We now have a closer relationship with the Lord. David and I are closer to each other. I feel more than a woman, in fact when I look in the mirror I see a beautiful young lady. Shania gives us more love and joy each day than we can possibly give her. We thank and praise the Lord for answering our prayers and for the fulfilment of our dreams. We have more than enough proof that what seems impossible for man is possible for the Lord.

'Weeping may remain for a night, but rejoicing comes in the morning' (Ps 30:5).

Another person who can testify to God's unfailing power is Ken Haynes. About fifteen years ago he was injured while trying to arrest a drug suspect. At the time, he was a police officer in southern California. The injuries he sustained were to his right arm, shoulder, neck and back of his head. Before he was healed he suffered from migraine headaches that became more and more severe as the years went by.

'It was a severe enough injury to force me to leave the police department, and I moved to Portland, Oregon seeking work in the computer industry.

'About two years ago the pain became constant. Each day I was in terrible agony and at least two or three times a week I was rushed to the accident and emergency with pain so bad I was throwing up. During these episodes I was extremely sound sensitive, and even the sound of someone breathing in the same room was excruciating. After going through what seemed like the entire medicine chest, the doctors put me on 130mg of oral morphine just to keep the baseline pain levels low enough for me to function.

'My wife, Kelly, had been praying constantly for healing and relief, but it seemed that, like Paul, this was to be my "thorn in the side" that I would have to bear for the rest of my life. Though despondent, however, we never gave up hope of finding a cure, or that the Lord would heal me. We continued to press with prayer and ask the Lord for guidance and healing.

'One day I read an article in one of the headache journals I subscribe to, about a condition known as cervicogenic headache (CH). It is a headache caused by an injury to the neck. This is a common headache among whiplash victims of car accidents.

'I searched high and low for a doctor in my health maintenance organization that knew anything about CH. No one seemed to know anything. I printed article after article, that I could find on the Internet, and took them to my doctors and specialists in a vain attempt to get them to try and diagnose and treat my condition. Each of them dismissed my reports and told me that they knew best what to do.

'Over the Internet we found a clinic in Toronto, Canada that seemed to know something about CH. I called them, and they said that I would have to travel to the clinic in order to get a diagnosis. We prayed, "Lord, if it is your will for us to go to Canada, would you please make it possible?" We put the word out to our friends that we were thinking about going to Canada to get the diagnosis done and asked them to pray that the Lord would open doors of opportunity for us to be able to go.

'A friend called us a couple of days after we'd put out the prayer request, and told us that their boss had accumulated enough frequent-flyer miles that he could provide us with two first-class, round-trip tickets to Toronto at no cost to us! We were flabbergasted! He also said that since he travels to Toronto on a regular basis, he has an apartment there. He normally would be there during that period of the year, but it just so happened that he would be on vacation in another part of the world, so we could have his apartment to stay there, rent free! WOW! What a miracle and a wonderful blessing! That's miracle number one.

'The Canadian doctors told us that we would have to be there for a couple of days, and that it would probably cost us around $2,000 to be seen and obtain a diagnosis. Unknown to us, some other friends had been collecting money for us to purchase an airline ticket. We'd expected to have to take out a loan for the trip expenses and doctor visit, and we were willing to do that, but the Lord had other plans. As it turned out, several other friends sent money to us. The total amount of money collected completely covered our expenses, including food, the rental car, and even the $2000 cost of the doctor visits for the diagnosis! That was miracle number two.

'We went to Toronto, and got the diagnosis. It was confirmed. I had the condition. The doctors in Canada told us that there was a good doctor in the US (in Minneapolis) that would be able to take my case. We decided that the Lord had obviously put us on this path and we were going to see where it was going to lead us. We made up our mind that we would go to Minneapolis. We didn't know how we were going to get there, but we were sure that if the Lord wanted us going to Minneapolis, he'd find a way.

'When we were on our way home, we found out that we could catch an earlier flight if we hurried. Excited to get home earlier, we jumped at the chance. We caught our connecting flight in Detroit and were on our way home. On this flight – that we really shouldn't have been on – I struck up a conversation with the gentlemen in the seat across the aisle from me. I found out that he was going home after being in the Caribbean for a week or so. He was a personable gentleman, and being polite, he asked me where I'd been. I told him that I'd been to Toronto for medical reasons. He seemed curious about what medical condition I had, that caused me to go all the way to Toronto to get a diagnosis. I told him about what I'd learned about CH and that the only people I could find to do the diagnosis and treatment were the folks in Toronto. He asked me if I was going to have a particular type of surgery done to correct the problem – which took me completely by surprise because it was the correct type of surgery. I asked him what he did for a living, and he told me that he was a doctor at the pain management centre at the Oregon Health Sciences University in Portland, Oregon, and that he was very familiar with my condition, and could probably treat it as well. That was miracle number three.

'Needless to say, I was very excited. I got his name and number and immediately took the diagnosis from Canada and the doctor's name back to my Health Maintenance Organisation to ask for a referral. The doctor from the aeroplane even supplied me with further published articles (that my doctors actually read!) that supported the diagnosis from Canada.

'After some red tape (that the Lord cut through quickly), I was in the doctor's office that I'd met on the plane and he was doing further (more specific) diagnosis to determine exactly what type of treatment I would need.

'Soon, it was confirmed by Oregon Health Sciences University that I had CH and determined that I would need a C2 Dorsal Nerve Root Ganglionectomy. I was referred to neuro-surgery for the operation.

'I am very confident that God orchestrated this whole series of events, so that I would get to the right people who could take care of me.

'It took a lot of prayers and three or more miracles before God would, in his time, bring healing. Each time God was able to display new paths over what before had seemed 'desert' ground.

'And we know that in all things God works for the good of those who love him, who have been called according to his purpose' (Rom. 8:28-29).

In 1979 Miriam Perry was diagnosed as having systemic lupus erythematosus. Hers was a three-pronged illness with symptoms in the collagen and immune system and a form of arthritic disease affecting the entire body. She explains:

'My muscles and joints, all the body tissues and organs, including my brain, heart and lungs were affected. The best way to describe my symptoms is to say that I felt like I had a very bad flu, with a fever, for over three and a half years. My skin could not be exposed to the sunlight for even fifteen minutes without severe pain. My stomach revolted every time I ate as the muscles needed to digest my food tried to do their work. My lungs stopped functioning at times, leaving me without breath, and my heart would race uncontrollably, leaving me exhausted. Besides these physical symptoms, I suffered from depression and an emptiness in my emotions that was truly the depth of my darkness.

'During this time God taught me from his word that I, that all of us, are dependent on him for everything: for our life, the very air we breathe, making it possible for our lungs to take a next breath. Even who I am is dependent on him. He taught me that he loved me and delighted in me, as I lay on my bed. It was not what I did, but who I was that mattered.

'On March 16 1983, my pastor at church called for a healing service. When I saw the announcement, I knew I wanted to be there. It was my 40th birthday, and I believe God gives birthday gifts. God gave me confidence that he would act through this service: expectation is a part of the healing process.

'As the service of prayer for healing began, I, and a number of others, came up to the altar area. I walked with what was jokingly called the "Perry shuffle". I needed assistance with the two steps to the altar. We knelt as the Pastor prayed general prayers and then he began to lay hands on and anoint one after another with oil and prayer. I had not knelt at the altar for several years because of the pain level. Now I was determined to kneel, though I almost passed out from the intense pain. The pastor came to me and laid hands on me. He prayed and anointed me with oil. Then he moved on to the next person. I felt no different. The pain was just as intense. I wondered if I had understood God correctly. I could do nothing to make the situation different. It was in the hands of God. I believed, but that wasn't enough. "Help thou my unbelief!" I cried with that biblical father.

'Pastor finished the prayers and excused us all. The person next to me offered to help me back down the steps. To this I responded in my pain "No, I am healed." With that fearful declaration of obedient faith I immediately felt a powerful surge of strength flow into my body.

'I leapt down those two steps and sat down by my son, Chris. Then I shouted: "Praise God! I am healed! I've got to do that again." So I ran up the steps and down again. By this time the reality of what had happened filled my whole being and I was filled with tears of joy. The service ended and my friends in attendance praised God with me. Afterwards I challenged Chris to a foot race to the car. I beat him. Just imagine, thirty minutes before I could only shuffle my legs because my hips would not move, but now I could beat my ten-year-old son in a fifty-yard dash. I was healed. The rheumatic fever which I had had since the age of twelve was gone. I have no symptoms of arthritis. There is no trace of lupus in my blood.

'The response of the doctors was sceptical at first. Now they say that I have a "good remission" since there is no cure for systemic lupus, except when final complications lead to death. At first they did yearly EKG on my heart, which had been damaged by the rheumatic fever since the age of twelve, to verify my improved health, as well as blood tests. There was no trace of damage to my heart. They continue with the routine tests, but now rarely even mention the lupus, I assume because they have decided that I am cured. Sixteen years of perfect health results tend to convince even the sceptical.

'I have put my hand in the hand of my God and yours, even Jesus Christ, the Great Physician, and I see his power at work every day.'

Miriam is now preparing to enter full-time ministry.

'Therefore, if anyone is in Christ, he is a new creation; the old has gone, the new has come!' (2 Cor. 5:17).

Chapter 7

Tragedy to Triumph

*And the God of all grace, who called you to his
eternal glory in Christ, after you have suffered a
little while, will himself restore you and make
you strong, firm and steadfast. 1 Peter 5:10-11*

The pain and turmoil caused when tragedy
strikes can often leave a host of unanswered
questions. Becoming debilitated as a result of an
accident or life-changing incident can bring the
victim to despair as he or she grapples with the
reality of a permanently changed life. In the
Bible, by contrast, we can read of a number of
characters whose life story tells of triumph over
tragedy.

Joseph was betrayed by his brothers, sold
into slavery, framed by a woman and sentenced
to prison; he emerged from prison to become
prime minister. Moses was rehabilitated from a
delinquent to become Israel's deliverer; Daniel,

from captive to counsellor; Job, from victim to victor; Paul, from persecutor to preacher. In all accounts God turned the tables, bringing strength in adversity and redeeming tragedy, showing his favour, that his name might ultimately be glorified through each one.

Doris Bebe, at the youthful age of twenty-one, received an injury that would change the rest of her life, but one that would also eventually lead her from tragedy to triumph. Her story is a testimony to the power of God even though it began with an encounter with the enemy.

'Early on in my high school career I began to hang around a group in school who listened to heavy metal. I began to sing songs like "Shout at the devil" and go to concerts that girls of fifteen should not be going to. I wore the Satan symbol, not realizing the consequences that this would have later in life. What I thought was just a cool thing to do had serious and significant meaning.

'One night at a birthday party I did the Ouija board and it said that I would die young in a car accident. That same year a friend and I went to a fortune-teller at a flea market and she said the same thing. Some five years later, a lady in a bar read my palm and all of a sudden she threw my hand away. I could not get her to tell me what it said, but she told my friend, who in turn told me. It was the same thing, but that this time I was going to die in a car crash at the age of twenty-one. At this time I was around nineteen. I thought I had plenty of time!

'Three months before my twenty-first birthday I moved back home to my parents. I thought that the second I turned twenty-one it would happen. As it happened I was not far wrong.

'Almost a month to the day of my twenty-first birthday, on October 7 at around 2:30 a.m., my life changed. I was out with a friend and we had just finished eating at Taco Bell. We ate in the truck. The last thing I remember was that I was putting the trash in the bag. Most of my recollection is based on what I was told by my friends and my grandmother because I have no memory of any of it – that was the Lord.

'A young girl of eighteen or nineteen had been drinking at a local bar. When she was ready to leave her friends tried to get her to stay and not drive. I was told she got in her car and drove away at high speed. She was driving somewhere around 85 miles per hour when she hit us head on. We were travelling around 40 to 45 miles an hour. I did not have a seat belt on and I was sitting in the middle. I was told that it was a very bad accident. There were four of us in the wreck all together. I was the worst injured and had to be cut out of the truck.

'They tried to do what they could for me but my injury was so great they needed to send me to a trauma hospital. The injury on my face was great. My cheek was peeled down and they had to sew my face up without any pain relief because they did not know at that time what the extent of my other injuries were. I was told that I yelled, screamed and cried very loud.

'The emergency room staff told my friends and family that they had never seen anyone with this kind of injury survive. They screwed a halo brace on me, a device that screws into your skull and is attached in four places – two in your forehead and two in the back. My neck was broken in the area where most folks die: C-1 and C-2. Well God had a plan.

'My first memory of when I woke up is of a group of people around my bed praying! I did not know who they were because no one I knew prayed! Apparently my friends and family asked for a minister who brought other church members to the hospital to pray. I believe that God answered their prayers even though they did not even know me. He knew me and had a plan for my life. I got home from the hospital fifteen days later. I had a brain concussion, a broken neck, and plastic surgery on my face. I also had bruising to my mouth. I lost half of my eyebrow and I had this crazy brace that went all the way down past my waist. Despite all this I did not feel any pain. I believe that Jesus bore the pain for me.

'I wish I could tell you that I was grateful for my life and the fact that I could walk but I was angry – very angry. I did not understand at the time why I should have been in the accident. God had saved me from death and from being in a wheelchair. No one would look at me and know that I had my neck broken. All of my life I had lived across the street from a young man who broke his neck falling off a trampoline, so I should have been very grateful. Yet I was bitter towards God. I knew he had saved me but I was angry that he'd let me live with the injuries. I remember feeling as though I had been ruined. Before, I had had a face with no scars and perfect teeth. I never even got pimples. Now I had lost part of a front tooth, I had big steel bolts coming out of my head, and when I went out in public, people stared. I wish I could say that I felt blessed to be alive, but I wanted to die.

'I was young and selfish. I think that during that time God tried to speak but I would not listen to him. I turned away and went on a road far worse than ever. I became cold and bitter. I began to drink in an attempt to soothe the pain.

'Through all this God never left me. He attempted to reach me in many ways. He allowed me to make mistakes and search for love and acceptance on my own. Then he pointed me towards the road I am on today.

'I am so glad he never gave up on me and continued to speak into my life. Though I became a very tough person, he has continued working to soften me up. I just want to thank God for the journey he has taken me on; it has certainly been an interesting one! I am so grateful for the things he has allowed to touch my life. I will shout and tell the world of all he has brought me through!'

Today Doris lives each day to the full. She is now married and a mother of four and has become an active member in her church fellowship. God taught her to enjoy what she has. Her prayer is simply to be used as a vessel from which the love of God can flow.

'Though you have made me see troubles, many and bitter, you will restore my life again; from the depths of the earth you will again bring me up. You will increase my honour and comfort me once again' (Ps. 71:20-21).

Marie Asner believes it was through the persistent and fervent prayers of her mother that she was healed from the effects of an accident that could have ended a promising career before it had even started.

'My mother was a musician. Not just any musician, but a church organist, piano instructor and keyboard-player in a dance band. Somewhere between my conception and birth, my mother decided I was to be a musician too. I was taken with my mother to rehearsals, whether they were in a church or band setting, and lay in my bassinet by the piano when she gave lessons. At age three, I showed musical acuity by pounding out Hoagy Carmichael's "Old Buttermilk Sky" with both hands. My parents were proud and sure I was going to be a musician of worth.

'The unexpected happened at age five. Before beginning formal lessons, my left hand and thumb were crushed when a car door closed on them. The wind blew the car door shut while I was trying to climb onto the back seat. Searing pain ran from my fingertips to my elbow. I screamed and screamed. Someone wrapped a cold compress around my hand and I was hurriedly taken to the nearest hospital. My mother alternated between crying, "Why, Lord, why?" to repeating, "...have faith...have faith." When we arrived in the hospital parking lot, she closed her eyes, raised her hands skyward and then, clasping my hand gently, wrapped them around the cold towel. Speaking softly, she said, "Hear my prayer, Lord."

'Through my pain at the hospital, I could hear doctors speaking to my parents: "Her hand is crushed and her thumb will probably never be moveable. It will be frozen in place. There is nothing we can do except put the hand in a cast.

She is right-handed and will go through life fine."

'This was not acceptable to my mother. She phoned our minister from the hospital, plus her friends and asked them to call their friends. Everyone was to pray for my hand to heal so I could be a keyboard musician for the Lord.

'My left hand was in a cast for six weeks. I managed well with my right hand and didn't miss playing the piano at all. At times when I came into the kitchen, I caught my mother in silent prayer and would tiptoe away, not quite sure what to do.

'It was time to remove the cast. I wiggled all fingers, including the thumb, which to me seemed normal. My mother was elated. The doctors had surprised expressions on their faces, then one sat quickly down in a chair upon seeing the new x-ray. It showed a thumb joint that was clearly not aligned, yet I was clearly able to use my hand! I soon began to practise the piano and take formal lessons.

'In the years that followed, I would not be a concert pianist, but I became a church organist, accompanist and piano teacher. The power of prayer healed my hand and allowed me to become a church musician. God has changed my life from potential tragedy to jubilant triumph.'

Today Marie has just retired from being an organist after forty years of service. Her left hand still doesn't look 'normal' but it obviously hasn't stopped her in the least. That day in the hospital parking lot God heard and answered her mother's prayer.

It's the attitude of thankfulness, in acknowledging God's power to protect through near-death experiences, that Barbra adopted when she recalls the life-threatening experience of her daughter.

'At the age of fifteen Kathleen was too young to seriously date, but she did have a boyfriend. One evening, when I was leaving to pick up my son, Paul, from baseball practice, she asked if she could just go with her boyfriend to pick up his little brother from a friend's house. She said they would come right back. I said, "All right, just make sure you wear your seat belt, and come right home."

'It was my father's birthday and my youngest daughter Therese was already at my father's house waiting for us to come over with the cake I had yet to pick up from the store. I left to pick Paul up at school, but decided to take the highway, rather than the shortcut along the back roads.

'After leaving the school, Paul and I ran into the store for the cake and some last minute goodies. As we were getting in the car, we heard and saw paramedics, fire trucks, three ambulances, and a multitude of police cars. I got a sick feeling in my stomach and said to Paul, 'Somebody needs our prayers, quick.' I wondered if there was a fire or a bad car accident. At one of the intersections I had to stop to let more emergency vehicles through, and I prayed, "Lord, those people need you right now, go to them and place your protective hand over them."

'We stopped at my parents, to drop off the food, before going home to pick up Kathleen, but my father met me at the car and told us to delay the party because Therese had fallen asleep. "Which way did you go to the school?" he asked, "There was a bad accident on the back road; I heard someone was killed. It happened just about the time you had to pick up Paul at the school and I know you always go that way. I was so happy to see you pull in, I had a gut feeling it was you."

'As Paul and I drove the short distance home, I could see our house was dark and when Kathleen is home alone, she always burned every light. As I turned off the ignition, tears fell, "It was Kathleen," I told Paul, "I know it." I ran into the house and checked our answering machine; no one had called. I breathed a sigh of relief, thinking that someone would have called by now. "Paranoid", that's what they always called me, and that's what I was telling myself, "You're just paranoid!" Then the phone rang. It was Kathleen's friend's mother, who worked in the emergency room of our local hospital. She told me that the three of them were in an accident and were being transported to the hospital.

'I didn't call my husband at work, nor my parents. Paul and I just left for the hospital. As I pulled into the parking lot, one of the paramedics, someone we have known for years, met us at our car. "I'm sorry, I'm so sorry", he said, with tears streaming down his face.

'The next thing I remember was talking to the doctor in the hallway of the emergency room. He asked me if I believed in God, and with that my knees gave way. "No," he said, "you don't understand. Do you believe in divine intervention?" I stammered a weak "Yes", not having a clue what he was talking about. He smiled at me and asked, "Do you know what shirt your daughter is wearing tonight?" I shook my head. He told me to go down the hall and look. "Your daughter is blessed with angels and so are you. From what the emergency personnel told me, there is no way that your daughter should be alive, let alone only have a few scratches."

'Kathleen was lying on a bed, waiting for more x-rays. When I got to her we both sobbed. As I was hugging her I had the urge to check her shirt; unzipping her jacket I read the words, "Jesus Saves". I knew then what the doctor had meant. All three were treated and released. On the way home that night, Kathleen told me the story:

'"It was really weird, but about a quarter of a mile before the accident, I said, 'Wait, we forgot to put on our seat belts; my mother will kill me.' Then a car was coming towards us in our lane, he swerved, and I knew we got hit on the passenger side of the car, where I was sitting. We got hit a total of three times because the car kept spinning in a circle. I felt his little brother's hand on my shoulder, holding me tightly in place. But Mum, after it was all over, I could still feel the hand on my shoulder. I looked and his little brother had flown out the back window of the car, as we later found out, on the first spin. It was an angel, Mum, I know it!" I knew it too, especially when we went the next day to look at the car, it had been split in half, right underneath my daughter's seat.

'Witnesses said the driver of the other car, was travelling ninety to ninety-five mph and the point of impact at that speed was directly at Kathleen's door. The police report stated that the car door was found fifty feet away from the scene of the accident, with the seat belt attached. So when the door broke loose "the hand" was the only thing that saved my daughter's life. The Lord knew long before I did that my child was in trouble, and I will always praise him for saving her life and restoring mine.'

'For he shall give his angels charge over thee, to keep thee in all thy ways' (Ps. 91:11 KJV).

Chapter 8

From Victim to Victor

Now to him who is able to do immeasurably more than all we ask or imagine, according to his power that is at work within us… Ephesians 3:20

He had been a victim of his circumstances since birth. He always believed, as he was told, that his blindness was a direct result of sin. Since birth he had lived with the constant reminder that he was paying the penalty for something he or maybe his parents had done. But when the disciples asked Jesus who was at fault, he took the opportunity instead to challenge their narrow-mindedness and explained, 'This happened so that the work of God might be displayed in his life' (Jn. 9:3).

All healing is a demonstration of God's power displayed in the life of the believer. It is God to whom the glory and honour must be returned. Healing ought to draw men's attention to the healer rather than the healed. It is for God's purpose, for his name to be ultimately magnified, that such miracles are allowed to take place.

Jesus sought to release the blind man from both the spiritual and physical darkness into which he had been plunged. 'Go,' he told him, 'wash in the Pool of Siloam.' So the man went and washed, and came home seeing (v. 7). His testimony: 'One thing I do know. I was blind but now I see!' (v. 25). I was a victim trapped in a world of spiritual and physical darkness, but now I have received victory from the Light of the World.

Sharon Bailey was also a victim. She sat in the doctor's office, shocked. She had just come in for a routine check-up. Of course, she knew about the lump, but she hadn't worried about it – after all, she was only thirty-two years old and healthy. The word 'cancer' had never occurred to her. Before the week was out, she was immersed in the world of a cancer victim.

'Victim. I hated that word. One afternoon, as a team of doctors bombarded me with treatment options, I asked them to leave. In the quiet of that small, sterile room, I began to talk to my best friend and Saviour. "You've always been there for me", I whispered. "I know this time it will be no different, but I need you now more than I've ever needed you before." His peace flooded the room and I called the doctors back in, ready to face what would come.

'That peace was a constant through the next few days. The news continually got worse. Not only did I have breast cancer, but also the tumour had spread to my lymph nodes. I felt as if I were on the outside looking in as they rolled me from room to room to a new set of needles and tests. One test revealed an ominous shadow on my brain. That night the doctors filed into my hospital room. Their faces were sombre. They spoke in whispers as if it would soften the news. Statistically my chances of survival were rapidly going down. If this shadow proved to be cancer, my chance of surviving five years had just plummeted from 40 per cent to 10 per cent after radical surgery, chemotherapy and radiation.

'They left the room and my husband and I sat wrapped in our grief. My children were young. I watched my husband as he wrestled with the news. I felt it was important that I share my wishes with him. The doctors had not been able to promise I would emerge unscathed from surgery on my brain. The shadow loomed over my central vortex – home to my memory, sight, and those abilities that make you who you are. As I began to tell him things about our children, our finances, my funeral, he closed his eyes. He stood and picked up my worn Bible. Opening it to 2 Corinthians 4, he began to speak the words over me:

> But we have this treasure in jars of clay to show that this all-surpassing power is from God and not from us. We are hard pressed on every side, but not crushed; perplexed, but not in despair; persecuted, but not abandoned; struck down, but not destroyed.

As he read, the words began to penetrate. I closed my eyes and began to silently worship the one who was bigger than me, bigger than cancer. My husband began to weep and worship God. The Spirit of God filled our room and we praised him for hours, singing and crying and even smiling at the tangible presence that filled the room. Nurses, who knew the news we had just received, tiptoed in and then back out, not understanding, but respecting our time alone with God. Hours later, I fell into a deep, peaceful sleep.

'The next morning they wheeled me down the hall. They wanted to get a clearer picture of the shadow they had seen the day before. They said it would only take thirty minutes. Two hours later, I was still confined in the metal tube. My husband was in the room with me; his only contact was my bare feet sticking out of the tube. But I would hear him – still praising God as the MRI took pictures of my brain.

'Hours later, I was surrounded by my family and many friends from my church. A doctor rushed in, still in his street clothes. "It is clear," he shouts, "it's gone." My husband slides down the wall and begins to weep while we celebrate. It was the first of many miracles over the next year.

'Believing that if God had performed a miracle I did not need treatment, I fought against my family. In the end, they won, and instead I fought against anger the day I sat in the vinyl chair waiting for them to slip the needle in my vein. The Lord spoke to me and asked me to trust him. "Let them know you are the one who healed me", I prayed. The nurses told me what I was to expect: nausea; hair loss; weakness; weight loss; the list went on. I felt the toxins hit my system and watched as my skin paled. I began to pray. "Help me make it through this hour", I said. Each hour I prayed again. That night I went home and continued to pray, not stopping for the next nine months as I went through chemotherapy and radiation. The doctors were amazed each week when I walked through their door, my long hair intact. I never shed a pound, in fact I gained. I soon became bored staying at home while my family was in school and at work and it was not long before I was back at it myself. Each week I sat in the chair, surrounded by others who struggled against the devastating effects of chemotherapy, and prayed for them. My long, curly hair, which reached below my shoulders, was a reminder that God was in the house. I could always see the chemotherapy hit my system. Within an hour, my skin would be almost see-through. My veins on my chest and arms looked like slender blue rope, yet I did not feel anything.

'It seemed as if God revealed himself daily in small ways, but often also in major ways. My family knew I was in God's hands and that they were seeing a miracle in progress. I worked each day and on Fridays only a half-day, going to my weekly chemotherapy session. I was a youth sponsor in my church and many times would go to a Friday youth retreat or fun night only hours after my treatment. With my hand bandaged, I would play volleyball with the teenagers. Several of the teens had promised to shave their head if I lost my hair. They praised God with me when they realized it was a promise they would not have to keep.

'One day the doctor's office called. I had gone in for my weekly laboratory work. My white cell count was low and my immune system seriously weakened. They told me to leave work and stay home. It was flu season and exposure to the current strain of the flu could take my life. That afternoon my children climbed off the school bus. I watched them struggle up the sidewalk, their faces flushed, their eyes heavy. They had the flu. I rocked, bathed, and ministered to my children until my husband came home. Within hours, he too was sick and running a high fever of 104. I called the doctor who asked me to come immediately to the hospital. I stayed home with my children, wrapped in the assurance that God was with me. I took care of my family for the next three days and never came down with the flu. It seems as if God himself had decided to be my immune system that week.'

It's been eight years now. Sharon shares how she now walks five miles a day. She reflects, 'I think the biggest miracle is that I have never felt like a cancer patient. I believe I have been through a battle, but God brought me through, fighting fear, and overcoming overwhelming odds.'

One day Sharon asked her doctor, 'When will you decide I am cured?'

He shook his head. 'Remission is declared after five years, you are cured after ten, but I decided you were out of my hands a long time ago,' he said. 'I have watched as patients whose cancer was much less invasive than yours lost the battle. I believe you have been cured for a very long time.'

'Because you have been my help, therefore in the shadow of your wings I will rejoice. My soul follows close behind you; your right hand upholds me' (Ps. 63:7-8 NKJV)

In early March 1998, when Gail felt a lump in her breast, she ignored it, and told God that this could not be so. Gail didn't tell anyone for fear of being told to go to a doctor. 'Perhaps if I ignored it, it will go away', she thought.

'I did, however, talk to God often. I say "talked" because the conversation was one way. I told him this could not be happening, that he was making a mistake. This continued for a month. In early April, finally consumed with fear, I talked to two friends who had experienced breast problems. These conversations scared me into making an appointment with our family doctor.

'My doctor examined me and ordered x-rays. She seemed to think that everything was all right. Now, when I talked to God, it appeared he was doing what I wanted, because everything seemed fine. I still wasn't listening, and that is the most important part of prayer. After seeing my doctor, I told my family and some Christian friends about the lump. They all began praying with and for me.

'The results of the x-rays came back with the news that there were not one, but three tumours, suspicious in type. My doctor immediately referred me to a local surgeon. This, of course, was not my idea of God's planning. I told God that I couldn't do this; I didn't have enough faith.

'Instead of seeing a local surgeon, I fought with my health insurer to see a surgeon who specialized in breast tumour surgery. I am not usually one to fight for something I want, but for some reason, this time I did. They finally approved it, but this doctor could not see me until the end of the month.

'At the end of April, I saw the specialist. He recommended immediate surgery, but I put it off until the end of June. About three days before the scheduled surgery, I hit bottom. Finally, with an open heart, I asked God to do his will for me in this situation. I cried out to him that if breast cancer were his will, I would accept it, but if not, then "let this cup pass from me". I physically reached out to him, knowing that only he knew best. At that point, I experienced a burning in my breast, something not really explainable. I didn't put much trust in the physical reaction, but I did know that I surrendered my will to him that night.

'On the day of the surgery, my husband took me to the radiologist's office to have a mammogram, an ultrasound, and have dye injected into the tumours so they could be more easily seen by the surgeon. After this process, I was to go to the hospital for the surgery. This should have taken about an hour. The nurse spent that hour using ultrasound, trying to find something in the breast that resembled what showed on the original x-rays. The radiologist finally came in to see if he could find anything. He found nothing. He tried to get fluid out of the "tumours", but with no result. This went on for two hours.

'I knew something was going on, because I could overhear the conversation between the nurse and the radiologist, but I didn't put two and two together. Finally, the hospital called, wanting to know where I was. My husband, waiting in the reception room, heard the technician and the radiologist talking to the surgeon.

'I was told to get dressed and that the radiologist wanted to talk to my husband and me. We were ushered into an x-ray room where there were three sets of x-rays on the screens. The radiologist explained the difference between normal breast tissue and what a tumour looks like by using these three x-rays. He showed us the tumours in the first two x-rays and then what he considered a normal, healthy breast. All the x-rays were mine; the first two were previous ones, the third was the current ultrasound. He could offer no explanation. He just kept saying over and over that the tumours were there and now they were gone.

'The surgeon still wanted to see all the ultrasound results for himself, and examine me, since he thought it must be an error and that I would still need the surgery. So my husband

and I went to the hospital. I was still not sure what was going on. Could what the radiologist told us be true? The surgeon looked at the results and examined me. To his surprise, nothing could be felt in the breast or seen in the test results. God had removed this cup from me. All I could do was give him the glory and testify of his healing power.'

Gail learned an important lesson that day. Even if she had only the faith of a mustard seed, God could work. It was clear beyond words that the only thing required of her was to trust him. It was also very clear that he doesn't need us to accomplish any of his purposes. He loves to hear, and delights to answer, the prayers of the saints on behalf of others.

'The Sovereign LORD is my strength; he makes my feet like the feet of a deer, he enables me to go on the heights' (Hab. 3:19)

For Jennifer Coyle it should have been the most joyous time her life. She had just got married to her life-long best friend. After their honeymoon weekend, Jennifer and her husband headed back home, happy but completely unaware of the crisis that loomed ahead.

'I noticed a twinge in my hip that seemed like a hot coil at certain times, like when sitting or leaning. I tried to exercise it out but each day I grew more and more uncomfortable. A visit to the local chiropractor revealed good news: "It's not a major problem like a herniated disc or nerve disorder. I think with manipulation and old-fashioned walking, you'll be fine."

'I followed his advice and visited him faithfully, but the pain continued to wear me down. A friend insisted that I visit her orthopaedist and an MRI was ordered. I was shocked. Indeed, the disc was severely herniated, my sciatic nerve was inflamed, and the doctor referred me to a neurologist. I couldn't stand, sit, or walk comfortably, and was nauseated by the pain a great deal of the time. My husband told me he was praying for me. "It would be better to find a cure," I sobbed one night, "I'm exhausted, sick all the time, and may be bedridden forever. If you want to leave me, I understand", and I cried my heart out. He took my hand and said we were in this for whatever was to be, and that prayer is essential in healing. Relieved that he was there for me, I didn't want to tell him that my spiritual life felt absent and that I just couldn't pray with him.

'Weeks of agony and sleeplessness wore me down; exercises and pain medication weren't leading to any noticeable change. The doctor recommended surgery when I was rushed by ambulance to the local hospital after a bout with crushing pain left me gulping for air. My husband, my friend, who for weeks slept on the floor next to me in the living room and whistled and sang as though he were holding up just fine, never showed me his terrified side. He couldn't imagine life without his active, vibrant new wife, who loved to wade the rivers fishing, take long walks and who enjoyed nature as much as he did. He prayed to Jesus fervently, asking him to relieve my pain but also to bring me to Him. He held my hand in the hospital as the nurse administered a strong and painful dose of pain medication. He asked me to pray with him and because I was too beaten down to object, I closed my eyes and asked God, "Where are you, don't you love me anymore?" Tears flowed as the emptiness and pain subsided and melted into a calm sleep.

'Two days before surgery, I noticed a definite improvement. I called the surgeon and was urged to come in. Taken aback, he admitted that I seemed to be healing to some degree, and he said the magic words: "Let's postpone the surgery; we'll see how you are in two weeks." I went into the vacant ladies room, knelt (not an easy stance at that time), and talked to my eternal friend, "Thank you and praise be to you! I know you wanted me to come to you after I thought I could do everything myself. I see the miracle, I thank you and I will never stop thanking you, and telling others about your powerful love."

On April 12 1998, Jennifer gave her heart to Christ, and was baptized in her local church. As the years have rolled along, she has enjoyed physical strength and activity. She is left with only a bit of numbness in her foot. It's a reminder that we are incomplete until we know God. It is our privilege to trust him with our very lives, and tell others about his healing power – a power that can transform us and give us victory in adversity.

'For everyone born of God overcomes the world. This is the victory that has overcome the world, even our faith' (1 John 5:4).

Chapter 9

Free in Christ

So if the Son sets you free, you will be free indeed.
John 8:36

I am sure we can relate to the apostle Paul when he says, in Romans 7:18-19: 'I have the desire to do what is good, but I cannot carry it out...what I do is not the good I want to do; no, the evil I do not want to do – this I keep on doing.' The cycle, familiar to many sincere Christians, of doing wrong, feeling the guilt and shame, being driven to repentance with a vow never to repeat the wrong and then succumbing once more to temptation, is a cycle of spiritual bondage from which every Christian seeks to be free. When we study the lives of the biblical characters we realize we're not alone. Many of them also struggled with this.

Healing from this vicious cycle was what Paul sought when he came to the conclusion that in himself there lay no power to contend with the selfish forces that emanate from within. His diagnosis – 'What a wretched man I am!' (7:24). The despairing prognosis – 'Who will rescue me from this body of death?' (7:24). The declaration of faith – 'Thanks be to God – through Jesus Christ our Lord!' (7:25). The conclusion – 'Therefore, there is now no condemnation for those who are in Christ Jesus, because through Christ Jesus the law of the Spirit of life set me free from the law of sin and death.' (8:1-2). God has made it possible for us to be free in Christ, free from the slavery of wrong habits and evil inclinations.

The powerful testimony of Don's compulsive disorder reveals how healing was achieved when he obtained freedom from the struggles and tensions in his mind:

'One October night in 1969, my mind just seemed to suddenly snap. I was overwhelmed by the thought that I might do physical harm to my children. I had been working as a psychiatric nurse at the time and was afraid that now I might be mentally ill myself. I was in the grip of what was then called Obsessive Compulsive Neurosis. The illness is now referred to as Obsessive Compulsive Disorder (OCD).

'OCD can take different forms. Some may have the symptom of compulsive hand-washing. Others feel the need to check things repeatedly, while others are continually filled with dread, simply because they feel they may have done something terribly wrong. And then there are those who are continually bombarded by repugnant thoughts totally alien to their nature, thoughts that can overwhelm and keep you on the brink of despair. Any of these symptoms can be totally exhausting.

'Indeed, OCD has been described as the most torturing of mental illnesses. Having a mental illness, despite living in a supposedly enlightened age, is not socially acceptable. This may be even more so in the Christian community than the secular. Many OCD people are fortunate, in that they seem so "normal". Because they know they're sick, they're able to hide it. And all the time they're hiding, the suffering goes on: which was how it was in my case.

'At the beginning of my illness, thirty years ago, the accepted treatment was psychotherapy, rest and medication (usually an anti-anxiety agent). I took a different approach. I did make three visits to a psychiatrist to confirm my self-diagnosis, but I had a family to support. I could not rest and I couldn't afford what might be psychotherapy.

'Rather than rest, I took on an even heavier schedule. I became active in my church and community, I worked hard at being a good husband and father…and I prayed. Like never before in my life, I sought God's help. With that, my Christianity took on new meaning. I came to see that it's not just a religion, but also a way of life.

'The next year was an unending struggle. I pushed myself out of bed each morning despite the depressed feeling that always hit at that time. I pulled myself through each day. Sometimes the thoughts would let up, only to come storming back again. It's an amazing thing that my job performance never suffered. I can remember many hastily murmured prayers, followed by a feeling that God's angels were looking over me.

'Through all of this I said nothing to my young wife. I was afraid – afraid she wouldn't understand. Had I been suffering from a physical illness, I would have shared my torment, but I was mentally ill, having thoughts about harming my children. I understood my illness and knew I would never harm anyone; but how could she possibly understand. Might she not begin to fear me and decide to take our children and leave? I know I could never have withstood such a loss. Besides, what a terrible burden to dump on the person I loved the most! I could talk to no one but God.

'As time went on, I began to climb out of the deep pit into which I'd fallen. My self-devised treatment plan began to work. I still had my rough days and the morning depression was still there, waiting to snare me. But once I got going with my busy day, the depression would lift. It was rather ironic that while people were continually thanking me for helping them, I couldn't thank them for helping me. Not only were they helping, but I was gaining a love for my fellow humans I had never before possessed. I'd also come to one other conclusion. God's healing power is available to the mentally ill as well as the physically ill, but we need to pray as if it all depends on God and work as if it all depends on us. Everyone will not be healed, and I can't explain why – but the same rule applies to all nevertheless.

'By 1974, the thoughts were tormenting me much less frequently. I felt free for the first time in years. I'd fought my battle with my secret disease and with God's help, had won. I thanked him for his deliverance. I might have lived out the rest of my life without anyone knowing how sick I'd been. But then, OCD, my bitter enemy, reached out to ensnare me in a way I was totally unprepared for. It was as if Satan was trying a new approach. Dr Judith Rapoport, whose book, *The Boy Who Couldn't Stop Washing*, is the best I've ever read on OCD, says a propensity for the illness is inherited. She further states that the most likely progression will be from father to son.

'My second son, John, had been a happy little boy who grew into a very idealistic young man. At the age of twelve, when other kids his age were engaged in pursuits of a trivial nature, John started a club to protect the environment. As a teen, when other kids were toting marijuana to school, John was carrying his Bible. While some teens were getting into trouble on Saturday night, John was attending church activities. We were very proud when during his senior year he announced he wanted to attend a Bible College and go into full-time Christian work – the first in our family to ever make such a commitment.

'When John graduated from college in 1982, things had never been better for my family. I seldom thought of the dark days of my illness. After graduation, John accepted a position with a Christian organization. It was then that things started to go wrong for my son. Perhaps it was his idealism that worked against him. Things didn't turn out the way he expected. I could see he was stressed, but I knew I could do nothing but pray.

'I saw him become irritable and angry. To add to his career difficulties, a series of relationships with the opposite sex turned sour. In conversations with him I got a sense of total frustration. If all he wanted to do was serve God, why was his life in such chaos? The worst was yet to come.

'John quit working for the ministry and began taking jobs far below his intellectual capabilities. I wanted desperately to help him, but didn't know how. Then one night he blurted out what was really bothering him. His words brought back all the horrible memories of 1969, only this time the pain was worse. It was my dear son who was suffering the horror of Obsessive Compulsive Disorder. If, at that moment, I could have taken John's suffering upon myself, I would have gladly done so. But one thing I could not do was admit the truth about myself. My illness was now part of my past. I wanted it to stay there, buried forever. It was a decision I would come to regret. On that night, I failed my family, my son and my God.

'I patiently explained to John that his thoughts were only that, he need have no fear of acting on them. I told him about OCD, that it was a mental illness and was treatable. He went into therapy and for a while things seemed to get better. He even got a position with a foreign mission and was out of the country for a year. His letters home made no mention of OCD. I wanted to think that he had decided to treat his illness the same way I did – by busying himself so that he'd have no time for unwanted thoughts. I prayed fervently that this would be so.

'When John returned from his overseas mission, he was expecting to get a stateside assignment with the same organization. During his initial interview, he did what we had always told him to do – he was honest. He was turned down because of his psychiatric history. It was a blow. He was good enough for an overseas assignment, but not good enough for his own country. He came home to decide what to do with his life.

'I would lie in bed at night and hear him crying out. My wife didn't understand, but I did. On Thanksgiving Day, 1987, John attempted suicide and was admitted to a psychiatric hospital. I now knew that my well-kept secret would have to be revealed. For twenty years, no one had known but God. When I told my wife, she held me tight, and cried. How foolish I'd been. I was married to a Christian wife who loved me. Why did I ever fear she wouldn't understand? Before the day was out, my entire family knew the truth. Our meeting brought tears, hugs and words of support. We were a family. We would now join together to help the one who needed it. John need have no fear of desertion. We held hands and prayed that John would be delivered.

'I was nevertheless apprehensive about my meeting with John in the hospital. Would he be angry because I hadn't told him the truth? John explained that while he was angry about having OCD, he in no way blamed me. I could not help having OCD any more than he could. With those words, a heavy burden was lifted from my shoulders. I had been carrying an unnecessary load of guilt. Parents want only to pass on good things to their children; I had passed on a disease. But John was right. I couldn't help it. God knew it and John knew it. I guess it just took me a while.'

It's been twelve years since this occurrence. Both Don and his son John have struggled much, but John's now married with a family of his own. He has a good job in the secular world and is a faithful member of his church. Don, who is now busy enjoying his grandfather years, concludes, 'Life has been good to both of us.'

'But you, O Lord, are a compassionate and gracious God, slow to anger, abounding in love and faithfulness. Turn to me and have mercy on me; grant your strength to your servant and save the son of your maidservant.' (Ps. 86:15-160).

For most of Vivienne Tsouris' life, she too has struggled with unreasonable compulsions.

'As a child I was compelled to do things in certain numbers. For example, if I blinked I was obliged to blink four times, or if I knocked my ankle I would have to make sure that the correct number of subsequent knocks was administered. Thoughts also needed to be brought into line, so that even after performing particular actions the required number of times, I invariably had to repeat the whole sequence until I was able to simultaneously think the correct thoughts. All this without anybody noticing of course!

'By the time I was married with a young family, constant hand-washing had become a major part of my routine. The rules were endless, but dead secret. If I awoke in the night I would creep around the children's bedrooms, touching each one on the forehead feeling like a ghost gliding about on its habitual nocturnal haunts. The hardest part was always getting through the bedroom door afterwards, stepping backwards and forwards through the opening as I endeavoured to control my erratic thoughts. Of course there were long periods of time when the compulsions grew less, and my habits became so much a part of everyday life that I scarcely noticed them; but during times of anxiety or insecurity my obsessions became unbearable. Prayer brought no real relief, and I was convinced that this was just an unavoidable part of my make-up.

'After the death of my parents I found my mind being taken over to an alarming degree. There were constant voices in my head which often felt like a battle-ground. I wondered whether there might be a way out of my obsessive behaviour, if only I could find it.

'One night as I lay in bed I was intrigued by a persistent mental picture which seemed to impress itself upon me. The image was a part of the inside of my brain, and there, attaching itself to the intricate convolutions, was a cancer. As I focused in on the vision I sensed God communicating some fascinating truths. As cancer cells tend to imitate and take on the form of the normal cells of whichever organ they are invading, so the obsessive compulsive disorder which I had been host to for so long had developed alongside of me. It had so successfully integrated itself within my personality and lifestyle that I had come to accept that this was simply the way I was. What God revealed to me in that instant, however, was that the disorder was a foreign entity and did not belong there. I prayed, not very hopefully, for further help, and eventually fell asleep.

'Because of the deep sense of peace instilled within me by this experience, I decided that, instead of engaging in my usual morning prayer time, I would just sit quietly and meditate for a while, listening to the Holy Spirit. Two scriptures came strongly to mind. First (Jn. 16:13), "When he, the Spirit of Truth is come, he will guide you into all truth", and second, (Jn. 8:32), "You shall know the truth, and the truth will make you free." I remembered reading that if we ask the Holy Spirit to lead us to the truth and root cause of a problem, he will do so. I could believe this happened to other people – but to me? Well, I would try.

'A few minutes later I was reaching for a pen and paper in order to list the many memories, pictures and words which came flooding into my consciousness. It occured to me that as far back as I could remember I had had a sense of being surrounded by a number of long, white spiritual beings who had a desire to participate in my life.

'At this point, before relating any more of my experiences under the Holy Spirit's guidance, I need to give some background information about my family.

'Two years before I was born my mother gave birth prematurely to a baby boy who lived for just four hours. She had been deprived of any physical contact with him and the experience had left her with deep traumatic scars and an unutterable sense of regret that she had never been able to hold the child in her arms. My birthday, March 28, was also the date upon which the baby had been buried two years earlier – a fact which would undoubtedly have seemed significant to a grieving mother.

'The list of dream-memories and associations which continued to flood my mind seemed endless. However, I eventually found myself puzzling over a vivid mental picture which for a while I couldn't quite make out. "What is it,

Lord?" I asked, intrigued. The answer came in a flash of revelation. The image was a picture of a birth – my birth! Now the fragmented thoughts, images and memories began to merge together to form a picture. I had always sensed that in my mother's eyes I had been a replacement, and to some extent, a measure of healing for the unresolved trauma. After losing the baby she had suffered several miscarriages and only succeeded in conceiving me with medical help. Obviously I was a much-wanted child. The picture suggested that even in the womb I had been affected by my mother's anxious concern. She was understandably prone to be over-protective, and so much so that she unwittingly invoked the intervention of spirit guides to take care of me, thinking that she was asking for the loving care of the spirit of my grand-father!

'Colossians 2:15 says that Christ, "having disarmed principalities and powers …, made a public spectacle of them", and "triumphed over them". Obviously Christ's resurrection from the dead is the ultimate triumph over evil. Those who have received the gift of his life are legally placed in this position of authority. So, in response to this amazing revelation, I thanked God for my sure salvation through Christ. I asked forgiveness for having participated in a relationship with demonic powers, albeit unwittingly. I renounced that relationship and all communication with wrong spiritual influences, and in the name of Jesus Christ commanded those spirits to get out of my life.

'Strongholds are mental habit patterns that have been burned into our minds over time, or by the intensity of traumatic experiences. In my case those habit patterns had been established over a period of many years but initially through the intensity of my mother's trauma as it affected me in the womb. Only the Holy Spirit could expose and unravel such a tangle of relational cause and effect. And only the Lord Jesus could offer the solution.

'I realised the power of Satan is in the lie, and in his ability to deceive. Once the lie is exposed our minds become free. I knew instantly that I had been released from mental bondage, but of course the habits took longer to break. Every time I habitually touched something I would think, "I don't have to do that any more." The sense of freedom was exhilarating.

'During times of stress or anxiety I have to exert extra resolve to keep my mind free, but the unalterable fact is that God's Holy Spirit led me to the truth which exposed Satan's deception. "You shall know the truth and the truth will make you free."'

Chapter 10

Peace of Mind

Nevertheless, I will bring health and healing ... I will heal my people and will let them enjoy abundant peace and security. Jeremiah 33:6

The relationship between mind and body is very intimate. When one is affected, the other sympathizes. The condition of the mind has great influence on the well-being of the body. Grief, anxiety, discontent, remorse and guilt all tend to break down the life forces and physically decay the body. By contrast contentment, thankfulness, joy, love and trust, all help to strengthen the soul. It was Solomon who said, 'A cheerful heart is good medicine, but a crushed spirit dries up the bones' (Prov. 17:22).

Such abiding peace and rest of spirit has but one source. It was of this that Christ spoke when he said, 'Come to me, all you who are weary and burdened, and I will give you rest' (Matt.

11:28-29). 'Peace I leave with you; my peace I give you. I do not give to you as the world gives. Do not let your hearts be troubled and do not be afraid' (John 14:27).

Job is an example of one who had such peace of mind. Even though he had lost all and suffered severe boils, he was able to say, 'The Lord gave and the Lord has taken away; may the name of the Lord be praised' (Job 1:21). There was no assurance that he would be healed but because he was secure in his trust in God he was prepared to face the future with complete acceptance of his conditions. 'Though he slay me, yet will I hope in him' (Job 13:15).

It was for mental restoration that Irene Carloni prayed when, at the age of 17, her son Mike, with his whole life ahead of him, was diagnosed with Multiple Sclerosis (MS). A once happy and content child became an unhappy, angry and rebellious teenager. Irene tells the story:

'My husband and I, along with our doctors, looked at many research programs that treated MS. Mike even participated in one research program at the local university. We prayed for physical healing for Mike and looked to our church for help. We went to several healing services but never saw any improvement. During this time I shed many tears. In my sorrow I found myself thinking about Mary, the mother of Jesus. How did she feel when she saw her son suffering? It was all too hard to understand.

'The years slipped by while I continued to pray for Mike's healing. Meanwhile Mike's anger and rebellious attitude continued to grow worse. I found that I, also, was becoming more impatient and short-tempered. One day during my prayers, I was prompted to give my son to the Lord.

'"Lord, I know you're in control of everything. I give you my son and I will accept whatever you decide to do with his life. Please help me to accept his illness and have enough patience to care for him."

'After praying that prayer I experienced a feeling of peace. In turn, that feeling of peace allowed me to see Mike in a different light. When he was angry I made jokes and sang silly songs instead of becoming angry myself. Gradually his anger slipped away. My husband noticed that Mike was happier and more content. In time, our daily lives settled into a pleasant routine.

'We asked the doctor about the change in Mike's personality. He told us that MS had affected Mike's memory and left him with a feeling of well-being. Secretly I smiled to myself. I knew that this was a healing from the Lord and an answer to my prayers. The Lord had healed Mike in his own way, and healed me as well.

Twenty-three years have passed since Mike was diagnosed with MS. Through God's healing, our anger turned to laughter and frustration turned to peace.

'You have turned for me my mourning into dancing; you have put off my sackcloth and clothed me with gladness...O Lord my God, I will give thanks to you forever' (Ps. 30:11-12 NKJV).

As Joan began her first day as a teacher, little was she to realize that one of her pupils, whose psychological disorder seemed disruptive, would take all the patience and love she could find to see him through.

'I thought he was just trying to clear his throat. But when he was still "barking" at the end of the first school day, I realized I was in for trouble. The "ark-arking" every two or three minutes was a distraction, to say the least. To compound the problem, the facial tics and contortions Benny manifested brought giggles and interruptions from the class all day long.

'On the second day of school I was prepared, I thought. I had anticipated every move and would be equal to the task. I would seat Benny adjacent to my desk away from the other students. This would be a disadvantage for him, being so far from the chalkboard, but I reasoned I could give him lots of individual help.

'It was a disaster! The constant "ark-ark" forced me to repeat instructions continually. Moving Benny away from the other children seemed only to make his barking louder.

'"Teacher, I can't hear. What did you say to do?" the children asked repeatedly.

'When the second day of school ended, I rushed to the counsellor's room in desperation. I learned a lot from Benny's psychological work-up from the year before. He had "alcohol foetal syndrome". There was no prenatal nutrition, plus unsuccessful attempts at abortion. Benny was abandoned at birth. He was being reared by a caring grandmother who had done everything she could to change Benny's behaviour and stop the barking and facial contorting. The psychologist's findings included the beginnings of Tourette's syndrome. The disease begins with facial contortions and tics.

'"Lord, I need help with Benny", I prayed every night. For the first time in twenty years of teaching I didn't know what to do or how to cope with this kind of situation. I prayed for wisdom daily. I knew the child had suffered from malnutrition, rejection and defeat. I resolved to bombard this child with prayer, to love him and give him the supportive, individual instruction he needed.

'Being a public schoolteacher, I could not pray out loud, but I could pray mentally and silently in the Spirit. In my mind I warred daily for Benny. The more I prayed, the worse Benny seemed to get. One day I was trying to teach the regrouping concept in math. The children were having a hard time grasping it, and the constant "ark-ark" from Benny made teaching almost impossible. Then a remarkable thing happened.

'I was standing before the class when I found myself saying: "Benny, come up here please." He stood beside me and I resumed teaching. He resumed "ark-arking". I put my hand on Benny's shoulder and silently prayed for him while teaching math at the same time.

In the weeks and months that followed, the same scene happened many times. Benny would bark, and I would stand him by me with my hand on his shoulder, teaching out loud, but praying for him silently. I was patient and obedient in what I perceived the Lord would have me do. I always knew children needed reassuring, but I didn't realize that my hand on Benny's shoulder was the touch he needed. Occasionally, I would pat his shoulder and that, along with prayer, was moving the mountain in Benny's life.

'Changes were so gradual that I hardly noticed them. I had either learned to live with the "arking", or it had disappeared so gradually I had become accustomed to it.

'One day in March one of my students exclaimed before the whole class: "Teacher, have you noticed that Benny doesn't bark anymore?"

'And then it hit me! The thought came: "That's right! I can't remember the last time I heard Benny bark. Hallelujah! Thank you, Lord!"

'I was even more ecstatic when a copy of Benny's latest psychological appraisal was given to me.

"A very definite improvement", the report read. "I don't know what you're doing," the counsellor had written, "but keep it up; it's something very right."

'It has now been four years since Benny was in my room. I have kept up with his progress.

'"How's Benny doing?" I casually asked one of his teachers the other day. "Does he ever make funny noises or weird faces?"

'"No," she replied, "but he told me something very strange the other day."

'"What?" I asked anxiously.

'"Well," she said hesitatingly, 'Benny says...he doesn't bark anymore."

'Do not be anxious about anything, but in everything, by prayer and petition, with thanksgiving, present your requests to God. And the peace of God, which transcends all understanding, will guard your hearts and your minds in Christ Jesus'
(Phil. 4:6-7).

The story of six-year-old Holly Godbehere (God-be-here) highlights the effect low self-esteem can have on a person's stability and peace of mind. Holly lived in the north-west suburbs of Chicago in a family of five. She came from a Christian family and a beautiful home, in a safe, quiet, tree-lined neighbourhood. The children, one boy and two girls, were active, along with their parents, in church and school activities. Holly was the youngest of the children, a little cutie with big China blue eyes, fair skin and lots of freckles. Her sister, Sally, who was three years older, was another beauty with chestnut brown hair, big brown eyes and creamy olive skin. Holly longed to have the flawless, freckle-less complexion of her sister, Sally.

As cute and sweet as Holly was, her freckles started to become a big problem to her. She hated those freckles and she complained and cried about them almost every day. She felt she could never be pretty like her sister as long as she had those freckles. Holly's mother continues the story:

'Even our pastor had to be gently asked not to call her "freckle face" at church on Sunday mornings as she cried all the way home. I saw her sadness and she seemed so unhappy. Could a six-year-old have depression, I wondered? This is ridiculous – we couldn't seem to convince her that her freckles were not important to

who she really was and that she was so special
to us. She didn't like them and she was angry! I
didn't know what to do. Her schoolwork
started to suffer and her teacher suggested a tu-
tor to help her in reading. Well, I soon learned
this was not just a passing fancy. It was a prior-
ity. I went for help from the only place I knew. I
turned to the Lord and prayed every day that
God would guide, direct, and give me the wisdom to solve this problem that was beyond me.
What should I do? How could I help my little
girl feel good about herself? As her mother I
could only let her know how very special to us
she was.

'My prayers were very decidedly answered
in no time at all. Within two weeks, we received
a letter in the mail from a modelling agency.
They wanted Holly for modelling. When we
read the letter to her, she felt so very special and
she felt good about herself. "My freckles aren't
so bad after all. It's a shame Sally doesn't have
any freckles". Two days after that, Holly came
home from school announcing that she had won
the United Way Poster Contest for her class and
would be a special guest of honour at a dinner at
a restaurant and her father and I would be her
guests. She felt so proud.'

Prayers for this mother and her little girl were
answered. 'Godbehere' (God-be-here). . .God
was certainly there for her. Holly was once
again a happy, beautiful little girl with a

precious light sprinkling of cute little freckles. Her story reassures us of the precious promise in Isaiah 54:13: 'All your children shall be taught by the Lord, and great shall be the peace of your children.'

With physical healing it's easy to see tangible improvement, but the healing of inner wounds, the ones that come from tragedy and emotional pain, is harder to guage. Brenda Nixon shared the healing of her father's 'inner wounds' sustained by reoccurring memories of World War II.

'In the 1940s our world was at war with itself. A seventeen-year-old American farm boy called Joe, to whom service was important, quit high school to enlist. By nineteen he had faced active combat with his platoon stationed in Okinawa, Japan. Horrors and atrocities no eyes should ever see left permanent scars on this young man.

'Following the close of World War II, he returned to his small farm safely nestled in the hills of southern Ohio. He was met, as were many, with a hero's welcome. Life to the returning solder was abundant with new possibilities and soon he found a job as a carpenter, a job God would use to bring healing.

'Years passed and Joe worked his way up to becoming a Carpenter's Foreman. His many responsibilities included hiring skilled carpenters for each job-site. The United States had enacted an Equal Opportunity law mandating the hiring of minorities. Many were interviewed and hired by my father who was noted as being a fair boss.

'His most heart-wrenching decision, one that would change the direction of two lives, was to hire a Japanese veteran of World War II. Known as "George the Jap", Joe's new hire soon proved his worth. He was a dependable, conscientious, hard labourer. The war years were far away and the emotional distance enabled the two to become acquainted. First, they exchanged facts about their family and children. Similarities brought them closer, so they shared about their childhood, and then their war stories. George admitted his inbred hatred towards Americans for invading his country. Joe confessed his feelings against the Japanese bombing of Pearl Harbor and horrid memories in Okinawa. The old wounds still caused pain, yet the two men found comfort in their friendship.

'As a flower unfolds to reveal its beauty, a friendship between George and Joe began to unfold. One day George questioned Joe's belief in God. His response led to a discussion of spiritual matters. Joe witnessed to God's forgiveness soon after returning from war, to God's love and power to change lives. He shared how prayer had made it possible to forgive those he fought against. George showed an increasing hunger for God's grace and forgiveness. The pain that plagued the two faded as things of eternal importance took place. Joe prayed for George's salvation. He wanted George to know God's grace. Old wounds were healed, but God's work wasn't finished.

'Suddenly and without warning, George was taken with a serious illness. His return to work looked increasingly unlikely as his fragile life began slipping away. Their friendship now in full bloom, Joe visited George daily at the hospital where he witnessed and prayed with him.

'From the hospital bed one day, George looked into the eyes of his American friend and asked to be lead to Jesus. Gently, Joe guided George in the sinner's prayer where he experienced true freedom. Once mortal enemies, two old soldiers embraced in joy as God's work was complete. The old mental wounds were healed.

'Do not conform any longer to the pattern of this world, but be transformed by the renewing of your mind. Then you will be able to test and approve what God's will is – his good, pleasing and perfect will' (Rom. 12:2).

Chapter 11

When Hope Hurts

Trust in the LORD with all your heart and lean not on your own understanding; in all your ways acknowledge him, and he will make your paths straight. Do not be wise in your own eyes; fear the LORD and shun evil. This will bring health to your body and nourishment to your bones. Proverbs 3:5-8

The Apostle Paul's unanswered prayer for his 'thorn in the flesh' (2 Cor. 12:8-9) reminds us that prayers are not always answered according to our own will. Paul says, 'Three times I pleaded with the Lord to take it away from me. But he said to me, "My grace is sufficient for you, for my power is made perfect in weakness."'

Spiritual healing – a deeper reconciliation between God and man – is the highest and most complete form of healing one can receive. It's at times when God seemingly fails to act that what we may ultimately be drawn to is a spiritual restoration with him. I realized this in a prominent way a few years ago when I myself was diagnosed with tuberculosis. I contracted the illness via a medical laboratory dealing with infectious diseases. Although I prayed sincerely for healing, there was no immediate miraculous answer. The physical cure eventually came through the prescribed means given by the medical team. Indeed God uses all means necessary for healing including the conventional remedies prescribed by our doctors today.

It was whilst I was in hospital during the early stages of my illness, however, that the Lord made me realize the absolute importance of total dependence on him. The ministry can often come with many pressures and self-defined expectations. It's very easy to become so absorbed in the work of spiritually feeding others that your own spiritual well can run dry.

During those days in hospital, the Lord lovingly reminded me, through his words 'the battle is not yours [mine], but God's' (2 Chr 20:15), that whereas I had come to think of myself as being indispensable to my church, the church really belonged to him. I was really just an instrument like all the other members, and whether I was there or not, God's church would still move forward.

I reaffirmed my commitment to God: to be led rather than to lead, to wait on him, and rest awhile if needs be, that I might be able to offer a more effective ministry in the future. My illness resulted in a healing far deeper and higher than the physical, for although I became cured of tuberculosis, I received a spiritual restoration that brought me to a place of even greater dependence on God.

In like manner Carol Ballensky was to learn that although she couldn't put right the events of her past, a fresh spiritual encounter with God would bring with it far more than she had bargained for.

'I instantly identified him when our eyes met in the lobby of my hotel. He was a handsome, well-educated businessman. His vivid, blue eyes and dark hair gave him away; he looked exactly like my brother. It was my dad. On the way to dinner that night, I looked forward to catching up on the last sixteen years since he had left us.

'He had left my brother and me when I was two. There were no memories to reflect on; I couldn't remember a thing about him. The only whisper from the past was a lingering desire and hope that some day he would come back and love me.

'After graduating from high school, I could stifle the desire to see him no longer. After much agonized soul-searching, I called and asked if we could meet. My palms were sweating and my heart felt like a jackhammer, but he was receptive! He had established himself, his home, his business and a new family in the Hawaiian Islands.

'As we were seated for dinner at an exclusive Island Country Club, I sat viewing the deep green palms against the tropical orange sunset. The air was balmy, the breeze warm and soothing. I wanted the beauty of that moment to last forever, but, the euphoric feeling was shattered in a moment. I looked at my father; he didn't have to say a thing. The look in his eyes told me he had no desire or intention of starting a relationship, especially one of father/daughter. We sat listening to the ukulele and the band happily singing. My heart felt as though it was breaking into a million little pieces. I wanted to cry. He was seeing me out of a sense of obligation, nothing more.

'I chose to hide my disappointment. As I looked at him, my frustration grew. All I could see was a man who appeared to be genuinely kind and generous. Why couldn't he accept me?

'Nearly twenty years after that first meeting, he actually agreed to meet me again. He had relocated in Las Vegas, only a few hours from my home. I was happily married and had two beautiful children of my own. My son and daughter were beginning to feel the absence of grandparents in their young lives. My only chance was to remind him of a great and awesome God who could restore any relationship, including ours. I knew he grew up in a Christian home. Family members assured me he professed to love God. I was ready to roll out the red carpet and invite him to be a long-awaited part of my life.

'I did not go to our meeting to demand an explanation; I was offering complete forgiveness for his choice to leave me with no father, no future. All I hoped for was a small beginning, even an inkling of interest in my children and me, the grandchildren he had never seen.

'I assumed our meeting would be brief and unemotional by nature of the place he suggested we meet: a smoke-filled, bell-ringing, clamouring, Vegas Casino. It couldn't get much more impersonal than that! But, I had a mission, I felt the Lord calling me to make one last attempt at reconciliation. I had prayed about it, and knew the Lord was directing me to speak with my father to share my story and my faith. I went with an open heart and an ocean of hope. I was sure he could find a place for me in his heart. It was risky, but God rewards the faithful; maybe my dad would change his mind.

'Feeling the tension rising, we made small talk and ordered lunch.

'Grasping for words, I stammered, "My family vacations near here every year, I've thought about calling and inviting you to spend a day boating with us – you could meet my kids; it's only an hour from Vegas."

'Instantly, I knew I had made a huge mistake. A look of horror fell across his face as he shook his head saying, "Well, as you know I am not very kid-oriented. I hope you realize this isn't your fault, but I can't look back, the past is too painful."

'It was then I realized; I really had come for an explanation. I felt my face contort; I tried not to cry. Tears streaming down my cheeks, I forced a smile, "I really didn't expect anything different, I just had to try one more time."

'I knew that if there was anything I ever wanted to say to him, I'd better say it in the next few minutes; so I drew a deep breath. "Dad, I want you to know, even though I don't know you, I love you because you're my father." His eyes narrowed in disbelief. "I wanted you to know what has happened in my life, and how God has changed me."

'As you know, mum remarried after you left. The man she married was a child molester." Now his mouth hung open in shock. I wasn't sure whether to go on, but realized I had no choice but to finish what I had started. "Because he was a deacon in our church everyone trusted him. He began molesting me when I was five. I ran away when I was fourteen. When they found me, they sent me to live with my grandparents because I revealed the ugly secret," I plunged on, "I spent my teenage and young adult years raging at the unfair world I was forced to live in. Dad, the first time we met, when you lived in Hawaii, I was a mess. I drank the whole time I was there. You saw the hurt child who hated the world; now my life is much different. After over ten years of self-destructive behaviour and running from the hurts of my past, I realized I needed professional help. With the assistance of a Christian counsellor I've begun the process of sorting out the tangled web of my past. I love the Lord and want to share with others the hope I've found. If it weren't for God I wouldn't be here today."

'As I shared my faith with him, I could see he wasn't buying it. I felt as if I was talking to myself. Distracted, I sensed he was in a hurry to leave. I gathered my things to go, but left one thing behind...my hope. It hurt too much to hope. Was it so unreasonable to ask for the love of my own father? Gripping the steering wheel with one hand and wiping the stinging tears with the other, I drove back to my hotel. I was through hoping for things that would never happen. I dreamed all my life of parents who would love me instead of hurting me. I put my faith in God, followed his every direction, and yet sustained heart-wrenching rejection.

'I began crying out to God, "Why do I love this man who doesn't love me? He doesn't even want to spend one hour talking with me. Why do I long for the attention of a family who doesn't care about me? Why does life have to hurt so much? Then, it was as if God was saying, "Carol, that's how much I loved you when you didn't love me back. I loved you when you didn't even want to spend an hour talking with me. I longed for you when you turned me away. The love you are feeling for your father, the pain you are feeling from his absence, is just a glimmer of what I feel for you, and the sorrow I experience in your absence."

'I thought of a verse I had discovered just months before, "though my father and mother have forsaken me the Lord will take me up" (Psalm 27:10 NAS). I was reminded that I have a heavenly Father who loves me more than any earthly father possibly could. I knew I must have hope to survive. For me, parental relationships had brought only despair, but Jesus promises to never leave, never disappoint, and never change.

'Jesus suffered unjust and undeserved rejection at the hands of people who should have loved him. He knows how I feel. He gives the hope of everlasting love despite the pain caused by those who have hurt me. He gives me the opportunity to overcome rejection in my own life because I choose to place my trust in him. Yes, the hurts of the past still need to be acknowledged and grieved, but he promises to comfort me through the lengthy process. I am confident that through Christ, my heavenly Father loves me completely. I am a daughter of the King! He gives me new hope, when hope hurts.'

'Be strong and take heart, all you who hope in the Lord' (Ps. 31:24).

Sharon also had a hope. Her son Justin was born hydrocephalic, in a vegetative state. Then the diagnosis was reversed; there was brain tissue...anything could happen. Justin might be a 'vegetable' or a 'normal child'. Sharon recalls how she fell to the floor in despair crying, 'God, is my lack of faith keeping you from performing a miracle on my own son?'

The answer she got was in the form of a scripture, 'By grace you are saved through faith ... faith is not of yourselves, it is a gift from God.' Justin survived for four and a half months instead of a few days. Sharon was to learn that sometimes our vision of healing is not the only way God answers. Instead, obtaining an accepting and loving heart spiritually healed her. In our correspondence Sharon revealed, 'I had to forgive God for not being who I had been taught he was and to get to know him all over again for who he is.'

Sharon's experience is a challenge to us all –
to know God more for who he really is and not
what we *think* he is.

**'"You will seek me and find me when you seek me
with all your heart. I will be found by you," declares the Lord' (Jer. 29:13-14).**

Ellen Bergh was another whose experience
deepened her understanding of God. Her story
reveals the truth that 'God's thoughts are not always our thoughts, neither are his ways our
ways' (Isa. 55:8).

'In 1980, after ten years of marriage, I left my
husband for someone else – the Lord. Our party
lifestyle had brought me to the gates of insanity
and death. God tossed out a lifeline and I
grabbed it. I announced my conversion to my
husband Clarence as he worked on our insur-
ance forms on my latest trip to the mental ward.
He shook his head, too shell-shocked to believe
my news could make any difference. But God
makes all the difference. My craving for escape
into intoxication or death began to lift. I clung to
God and avoided joining my husband in old
pastimes of alcohol and drugs.

'My recovery baffled him and he resented my
new sober companions. I began to see my marriage as a run-down piece of property that
ought to be abandoned. Focusing on all my hus-

band's shortcomings I prayed for God to change him. Over the next year and a half I launched an assault to convert this heathen. Deciding he was a captive audience in the bathroom, I left magazines and tracts. Over tea I shared my spiritual insights until his eyes glazed over. I became a pain to live with. Why couldn't he just get with it? When out to dinner, I nobly sipped my coke and watched with distaste as he ordered a beer to prove he didn't have a drinking problem. We had less and less in common as I had become so spiritual and he a true vulgarian.

'One morning, as I whined to the Lord, I sensed him ask me, "Do you love me?"

'I was taken aback, "Of course I love you Lord, you gave me a new life."

'"Would you do anything for me?"

'"Yes, yes, send me anywhere. What is it Lord?"

'"Love your husband for me. I loved you while you cursed me, will you do this for me?"

'Ashamed, I apologized and asked God for his eyes to see my husband. I'd fallen into such fault-finding, I had to visualize a neon sign on his head. It flashed "God's property, no tampering" – a caution light whenever I felt tempted to nag him. I prayed to detect things to praise Clarence about, to our mutual surprise. Trust grew in me through obedience to the Lord. I sensed a change was in the wind, that God was preparing my husband for something. But what?

'A few months later, his mother was diagnosed with terminal cancer. Several times, Clarence travelled to be by her bedside. He picked up her Bible, the same one she had read every morning of every visit to our home. He began to read in the hope of comforting her as she drifted in and out of consciousness. God used his faith, born out of hearing the word he himself read to his mother. The Lord was to bring Clarence into a new life just as his mother slipped out of hers.

'Later Clarence was to receive the personal attention, tailored to his needs, of the loving Heavenly Father. In time, I saw how short sighted I'd been. I had wanted my husband to become a Christian for my convenience. God loved him for his eternal destiny. Where I had been impatient for a quick fix, God knew a complete remodelling of our marriage would be needed. He had to bulldoze my old attitudes so that he might help us begin to rebuild on his sure foundation. When hope fades, he is the only third person in a marriage that can make it work.'

'If you remain in me and my words remain in you, ask whatever you wish, and it will be given you'
(John 15:7-8).

Virginia Baty was to learn that God not only heals our diseases but also heals from sin and its consequences.

'It was January 1978. The year had begun pretty much like any other. However, three weeks into the month, I discovered a lump on one breast. My first response was denial. Troubled thoughts ran through my mind. It wasn't cancer – it just couldn't be cancer, there's no cancer in my family. I couldn't even tell my husband. I could hardly get through the day, I was so afraid. Finally, I had to tell him, and he immediately insisted that I make an appointment with the doctor. I still rejected the idea that cancer was a possibility – there must be some mistake.

'The gynaecologist confirmed there was a suspicious lump, most likely a tumour. Even though it could be benign, I should see a surgeon as soon as possible.

'Following the x-rays, we discussed my situation and options. There was a tumour and the doctor wanted me to have surgery right away. I was still sure it couldn't be anything, and I knew a biopsy would prove that. I even asked for a week's reprieve since we had already planned a trip for the upcoming weekend to see some of our family two hundred miles away. The doctor reluctantly gave permission but insisted on scheduling the surgery for the following week.

'We went on our trip but the words that we
had just heard weren't far from our minds the
entire time. We told our loved ones and friends,
who all began to pray for me. Without the
knowledge of this prayer support, I am not sure
I could have gone on in the next few days and
weeks. Even as I signed the papers prior to surgery, there was no doubt in my mind, that I
would be OK. My surgeon was a Christian and
he prayed for me before I was taken into surgery, which was a real comfort. I was somewhat
fearful, but with my husband standing by, I
went to sleep fully trusting God would take care
of me.

'The surgery took six hours and a tumour the
size of an egg was removed, along with
twenty-four infected lymph nodes and leaders,
spreading under the breastbone. It was cancer!
The doctor indicated he didn't know if they had
gotten all of the infected tissue during the radical mastectomy. They even had to do a skin
graft from my leg to the chest wall. We were told
chemotherapy treatments would follow my recovery from surgery.

'It is at a time like this that you realize only the
prayers of God's people can help to carry you
through. "Therefore confess your sins to each
other and pray for each other so that you may be
healed. The prayer of a righteous man is powerful and effective" (James 5:16).

'It took four months to recover from my surgery. During this time, as I waited for chemotherapy to begin, I became very apprehensive. The Devil taunted me with fears, and I was quite unsettled. You know how the enemy works, "You would not be fearful if you really were a Christian." "Where is your faith, Virginia?" Finally after much prayer and counsel I came to realize my fears were only human and it was OK. God would see me through.

'I literally fed on God's word. "Fear not, for I have redeemed you; I have summoned you by name, you are mine. When you pass through the waters, I will be with you; and when you pass through the rivers, they will not sweep over you. When you walk through the fire, you will not be burned; the flames will not set you ablaze" (Isaiah 43:1-3). "Do not fear, for I am with you; do not be dismayed, for I am your God. I will strengthen you and help you; I will uphold you with my righteous right hand" (Isaiah 41:10).

'I underwent twelve months of chemotherapy treatments and had very little of the severe side-effects many experience. I was even able to work part-time that year. God drew very close to me through the reading of his word and my meditation on it.

'During my hospitalization, our youngest son, who was deep into a life of drugs, alcohol, and waywardness, was broken-hearted about

my illness. He kept telling me that he was the
one who should be suffering – he was the one
who had done wrong, why was I suffering? We
encouraged him to understand that trouble comes to the just and unjust alike. We continued to
pray, and as time went on, we began to see a
change in his attitude; finally, he made a decision to give his life to Christ. I truly believe my
bout with cancer was used by God to help bring
him to the Saviour. My son has now been a
Christian for eighteen years. Praise the Lord!'

God not only heals our diseases, but heals
from sin and its consequences as well. God's
healing of Virginia confirms that the challenges
we go through are often just the experiences
that give others the courage to go on.

**'Praise be to the God and Father of our Lord Jesus
Christ, the Father of compassion and the God of all
comfort, who comforts us in all our troubles, so that
we can comfort those in any trouble with the
comfort we ourselves have received from God'
(2 Cor. 1:3-10).**

Chapter 12

He's Able

Now unto him that is able to keep you from falling, and to present you before the presence of his glory with exceeding joy.
Jude 24 (NKJV)

'If I can only touch the hem of his garment, I will be made whole' (Matt.9: 21). It was a poor woman who spoke these words - a woman who for twelve years had suffered from a disease that made her life a burden. She had spent all her means on the remedies of her day, only to be pronounced incurable. But she had heard of the Great Teacher who was able to heal.

In making his way through the multitude Jesus came near to where the afflicted woman was standing. Again and again she had tried in vain to get near him. Now her opportunity had come. She could see no way of speaking to him. She could not interfere with the procession. Her only thought was 'If I can touch his garments I will be made whole.'

As he was passing she reached forward and barely touched the border of his garment. In that moment she knew she was healed. In that one touch her whole faith was concentrated and instantly her pain disappeared. In the midst of her anguish and pain, deep down she knew that when all others had failed Jesus had proved able.

Jan Clark is a modern-day example of one who sought that one touch of the master.

A plaque hangs in Dr Perry's Obstetrics/ Gynaecological (O/B) office. There is a photograph of a beautiful mother frolicking on a sandy beach with a little baby. Above the picture is the following inscription:

> On March 13th a year ago God saved my life.
>   It's true;
> For all your prayers and acts of kindness, I want to show my appreciation to you.
> The power of prayer is miraculous. This I learned first hand.
> The true meaning of love and friendship I now also understand.
> 'He is Able' is the song that still rings in my ears.
> I know it is God's love that will carry me through the years.
> 'This sickness will not end in death, it is to glorify God's name'

Is a special verse given to my family that now as
   my own I claim.
So thank you so much for all you did to help pull
   me through;
My family and I are truly blessed to have friends
   as dear as you!

Janet Cason Clark (March 1997)

An OB patient asks a nurse to tell her the story of
why this plaque is there. The nurse sits down
and smiles as she begins to share. It was given to
Dr Perry on the first anniversary of Jan's miraculous healing. This is Jan's story.

On March 12 1996, Jan had lunch with her sister,
Jill. They were both excited about the upcoming
birth of Jan's baby. Jan had to leave right after
lunch in order to make her appointment at 1:45
p.m. with her OB physician. This was to be the
first baby for Jan and her husband, Greg. Her
expected due date was confirmed by ultrasound to be April 15.

There were no complications during the
pregnancy until that day. During the office visit,
Jan's blood pressure was noted to be high. Her
diastolic blood pressure was noted to be at 90.
Jan was sent directly to Labour and Delivery (L
and D) for more accurate monitoring. Having
been admitted to the Delivery Unit, Jan's blood
pressure was monitored. All tests appeared
reassuring. Pregnancy-induced hypertension

was the diagnosis. Late in the afternoon, Jan and Greg were allowed to go home. She was directed to remain on absolute bed rest for the weekend.

In the early evening, Jan started feeling pain in the upper right side of her body. Greg rushed her back to the hospital. She was admitted again to the Delivery Unit. Her diastolic blood pressure was 90. Her physician began to treat the blood pressure with Magnesium Sulphate, which will usually bring down the blood pressure. Jan's physician wanted to review everything with new lab work, early the next morning. Depending on her condition, he would either induce labour or perform a Caesarean (or C-) section.

Over the next two hours, the blood pressure elevated to ~140/100-110 (normal being ~120/80). Jan continued to complain of severe epigastric pain. The decision was made to perform an emergency C-section.

At 2:27 a.m. Addison Thomas Clark was delivered. Greg and Jan had a beautiful baby boy. Showing them the abnormal placenta, the OB physician said, 'If Jan had in fact carried to forty weeks, Addison would have died. He was not receiving enough nourishment from his mother's body.' This was one of many wondrous miracles! He spared Addison's life, bringing to remembrance a song Jan had sung:

He's able, he's able,
I know he's able,
I know my Lord is able to carry me through!!

Jan would sometimes substitute the word 'us' for 'me'. She would sing the words to her precious baby in her womb, 'Yes, Lord you are able to carry us through!' It was always a sweet, tender moment between Jan and Addison, 'God is able to carry us through this pregnancy.'

The Lord did carry Addison through the pregnancy. He was taken to the Neonatal Intensive Care Unit (NICU) for observation because he was only 4 lb., 15 oz. and premature. Because the pain continued in the upper right side of her body and the blood pressure was up, Jan was kept in the Delivery Unit. After a few hours, Jan was rolled in the hospital bed into the NICU to see Addison. She and Greg visited and stayed with him for thirty minutes. How excited they were to have their very first baby! They were proud parents.

Moving to the Well Baby Nursery, Greg asked that Addison could be taken to Jan for his 9.00 a.m. feeding. Addison started to breastfeed. Being proud new parents, they were filled with such joy and excitement. They had such a wonderful family time together. After one hour of visitation, Addison was taken back to the nursery. Everything was as it should be.

Later that morning, a maternity nurse came in to give Jan her medications. She was complaining of progressively severe pain in her right upper side. Suddenly, Jan experienced a reduction in her pain. She told the nurse, 'I feel better, and the pain is not there.' The nurse discovered Jan's blood pressure had dropped dangerously low. It was now ~70/40. Her condition deteriorated rapidly.

The medical team rushed into the room. They worked fast with rapid efficiency. Arterial lines and central venous necklines were inserted. IV fluids were increased. Her blood count was quickly found to be extremely low. Jan was losing blood! She had an internal haemorrhage. Whole blood was administered, but Jan's condition continued to deteriorate. She was in profound shock. A decision was made to perform an exploratory surgery with the likely probability of a rupture of the liver, from HELLP Syndrome.

As Jan was being rushed into surgery, Greg was standing up against the wall of the hallway. He could hear Jan softly singing, 'I don't ever have to be afraid, Jesus takes care of me.' She called back to Greg, 'Raise my son as a Christian!' This might have been their last goodbye.

Greg did not know if he would ever see his wife alive again. Tears streaming down his face, he saw the surgeon running down the hall taking off his jacket. The physician explained to Greg and the family that he had never seen anything like this before. She was in a grave condition.

Having told the family of the gravity of her condition the nurse set up a room across the hall for the family. The devoted, praying family began pleading with God to spare Jan's life. They sent out prayer requests all over to friends and family. The intercessions of the saints began to go up before the throne of God.

During the surgery, it emerged that there had been a massive rupture of the capsule of the liver extending through the entire right lobe of the liver. The liver has a thin coating like 'saran wrap'. If it becomes too engorged by the HELLP syndrome, it will literally burst. That's what had happened to Jan's liver. The bleeding was slowed by applying pressure. For over one hour, the surgeon had his hand placed directly on Jan's liver to stop the bleeding. She received eighteen units of blood and blood products. Surgical packing was placed all around the liver, and small drainage tubes were inserted from the liver area to the stomach.

The surgeons hoped that the packing would stop the severe bleeding. The incision was closed with the cloth packings inside. There was nothing else to do. Jan was transferred to Surgical Intensive Care Unit (SICU), and placed on a ventilator.

After Jan was transferred to the SICU, Greg and the family had a conference with the surgeons. The surgeons explained that the subcapsulary layer of the liver had ruptured from the most severe case of toxaemia and PIH (Pregnancy-Induced Hypertension) that they had ever seen through all their years of surgery and deliveries. While toxaemia is often seen during pregnancy, the physicians noted liver rupture was rare and explained that the packing would have to be removed in 24 hours to prevent overwhelming infection. Jan was facing yet another surgery - the third in two days. They would not know Jan's prognosis until 48 hours from the time that the packing was removed.

Removing the packing would be extremely dangerous since bleeding could reoccur. Jan's sister Jill asked the surgeon, 'What happens if it still bleeds?' The surgeon told them that he didn't know what he could do. 'There is also a high risk of damage to her lungs, kidney and heart, because she has lost so much blood', he added. The final consensus of the surgeons was 'We are doing everything that can be done medically, but we need someone else to take care of this. She is not out of the woods yet'. She needed God to save her life.

The prayers of the saints were bombarding the gates of heaven. Jan and Greg needed a miracle. Prayers began to be answered. While Dr

Perry, Jan's gynaecologist, was walking down the hospital hallway, silently petitioning the throne of heaven to spare Jan's life, he felt that God spoke to his heart. He felt impressed that Jan would not die. While sitting in the lobby, Jan's mother and sister saw Dr Perry. They asked him whether he thought she would be okay. Dr Perry was able to share with them what his impression was from the Lord. He told them, 'I think the Lord has assured me that Jan is going to be okay.'

These words brought the first bit of comfort to a family in distress. They knew the Lord was able to spare Jan, but what was the Lord's will for her life? Respecting the sovereignty of the Lord, they pondered these words in their hearts. To hear those words, 'Jan will be okay', brought such peace and comfort to them.

The family was allowed to visit Jan in the SICU room for only a few minutes at a time. The ventilator was loud. Her physical body was swollen beyond recognition. Jan was so lifeless. Her colouring was greyish white - so white! It was a shock to the family to see her in this condition. She had always been so vibrant, so full of life. They had never experienced a health crisis in the family. It stunned them to see their beloved wife, sister and daughter in such a grave state. It would have been a test of anyone's faith. For Greg and the family, it was going to be a long night. They had to trust God.

Continuing the prayer vigil, Jan's mother said, 'I am going to wrestle with God all night just like Jacob. I am going to keep praying until I know the Lord has heard me.' During the night, they would alternate in prayer. They continued to plead with God to let Jan live. Their church pastor gave the scripture verse John 11:4 to Jan's mother:

This sickness will not end in death. No, it is for God's glory so that God's Son may be glorified through it.

For the second time, a word of comfort had come to them. Jan will live! Hope began to spring in their hearts. Word about Jan swept quickly through the hospital. There is something about hearing of a new mother fighting for and possibly losing her life in childbirth that makes for a 'silence'. It is usually a time of such great joy. To hear of a new father making funeral plans for his wife pricks at the core of even the hardest of hearts. Also, she was one of their very own. Jan had worked in the Well Baby Nursery for ten years. Employees were praying for her. People she did not even know very well. They would come to Greg and the family and tell them, 'We are praying'. Usually the hospital is a noisy, bustling place, but Jan was on the hearts and minds of the entire hospital staff.

There was silence in the hospital - a heaviness was in the air.

Meanwhile, Greg had had a ten foot banner made for Jan. He hung it up on the wall opposite her hospital bed. The inscription read, 'HE'S ABLE'. Greg wanted Jan to remember the song she sang to Addison every day before he was born. Being a nurse, she was conscious enough to know she was in serious trouble. Jan was told she would have to go back into surgery. She was disheartened, but remembering the words to the song *He's able*, she said, 'Yes, Lord, you are able to carry me through to live to take care of my son.'

At around 1.00 p.m. Jan was taken back into surgery. As she was wheeled into the operating room (OR) Dr Perry told her, 'I am going to pray for you during your surgery.' While clasping her hand to comfort her, he whispered into her ear as the anaesthetic was introduced, 'Jesus is here with you, don't be afraid.' Standing in the corner of the room, Dr Perry prayed throughout the entire surgery. The surgeons had to remove the packing around the liver to see if it would bleed. With the OR filled with surgeons and support staff, Dr Perry prayed as each of the packs were carefully removed.

As each packing was removed, the blood did not gush, it only oozed. With the removal of each layer, Dr Perry would silently say, 'Thank you, Lord.' The haemorrhaging had stopped. The team of surgeons were encouraged.

While Jan was in surgery, Greg and the family went into the waiting room and to the hospital chapel. There, they continued to pray and plead for the Lord to save Jan's life.

After the surgery, the surgeons counselled the family. 'If we could go 24 to 48 hours without major complications, we would feel a lot better about things. She is still not out of the woods yet.' Dr Perry told the family, 'I have never felt the power of God as I did in that operating room.' Jan was taken back to the SICU room, still on the ventilator.

While in the SICU room, one of Dr Perry's nurses, who had befriended Jan, came to visit her. She pinned a little gold angel on Jan's hospital gown. Jan would reach up and touch the angel for encouragement.

When Dr Perry came by to visit Jan, she gestured with her hand, and blew him a kiss, as her way of thanking him. When Greg came back from the Nursery to spend time with Jan, she would write out instructions regarding Addison. She instructed, 'Sing and have worship with Addison.' Her sister Jill would go down to the Well Baby Nursery and tenderly hold Addison in her arms, gently rocking and sing to him.

While lying in her bed, Jan's eyes would see the banner, 'HE'S ABLE!' She would remember the words to the song,

> He's able, he's able,
> I know he's able,
> I know my Lord is able to carry me through!

On the ventilator, Jan could not speak out loud, but would silently sing these words in her heart, 'Lord, you are able to carry me through to live to take care of my son.'

The 48-hour critical period came to an end. Jan was still alive! She did not experience any major complications. Her heart had not failed. Her kidneys had not failed. Her lungs had not failed. The surgeons told Greg and the family, 'Jan is out of the woods.' She was taken off the ventilator. It was as if the Lord answered the prayers of his people, as in Ezekiel 16:6:

> Then I passed by and saw you kicking about in your blood, and as you lay there in your blood, I said to you 'Live!'

God had proved able to carry Jan through from death to take care of her son, Addison. Greg and the family rejoiced. He's able!

Over the next week, Jan's condition continued to improve. She received more units of red blood cells and her blood pressure remained stable. Two weeks later, Jan was still weak but feeling better. She was discharged and allowed to go home. The Lord had saved her life. The Lord had in fact carried her through the very shadow of death. The ruptured liver following delivery is almost always fatal, with a fatality-rate of well over eighty per cent.

One year later, on March 13 1997, Jan and Greg dedicated room number two in the SIC Unit. During the dedication ceremony, most of the physicians and staff gathered together with Greg and Jan to remember the marvellous healing he had done. On the wall is an inscription, which reads,

'He's Able'

Jan wanted the story never to be forgotten. So when their own loved one is lying in the same SICU room, in the same SICU bed, they can open the Word of God to read psalm 56:13: 'For you have delivered me from death and my feet from stumbling, that I may walk before God in the light of life.'

Today, Jan and Greg are raising their three-year-old son, Addison. And on Jan's license-plate is the inscription, 'GODS ABL', declaring to the world, 'HE'S ABLE TO CARRY ME THROUGH!'

The nurse finishes telling the story. Smiling, the new patient says, 'He's able to carry me through too!' Patting her stomach, she walked into the exam room for her doctor's visit. All the while, telling her unborn child, 'This same God is able to carry you through too.

Appendix 1

Biblical Promises of Healing

'But I will restore you to health and heal your wounds,' declares the Lord (Jer. 30:17).

This is what the Lord, the God of your father David, says: 'I have heard your prayer and seen your tears; I will heal you.' (2 Kgs. 20:5).

If my people, who are called by my name, will humble themselves and pray and seek my face and turn from their wicked ways, then will I hear from heaven and will forgive their sin and will heal their land (2 Chron. 7:14).

Be merciful to me, Lord, for I am faint; O Lord, heal me, for my bones are in agony (Ps. 6:2).

Heal me, O Lord, and I will be healed; save me and I will be saved, for you are the one I praise (Jer. 17:14).

Jesus said to Jairus, 'Don't be afraid; just believe, and she will be healed.' (Lk. 8:50).

Dear Friend, I pray that you may enjoy good health and that all may go well with you, even as your soul is getting along well (3 Jn. 2).

He heals the broken-hearted and binds up their wounds (Ps. 147:3).

The Lord is close to the broken-hearted and saves those who are crushed in spirit. A righteous man may have many troubles, but the Lord delivers him from them all (Ps. 34:18-19).

Do you not know? Have you not heard? The Lord is the everlasting God, the Creator of the ends of the earth. He will not grow tired or weary, and his understanding no one can fathom. He gives strength to the weary and increases the power of the weak. Even youths grow tired and weary, and young men stumble and fall; but those who hope in the Lord will renew their strength. They will soar on wings like eagles; they will run and not grow weary, they will walk and not be faint (Isa. 40:28-41:1).

My flesh and my heart may fail, but God is the strength of my heart and my portion forever (Ps. 73:26).

I am bowed down and brought very low; all day long I go about mourning. My back is filled with searing pain; there is no health in my body. I am feeble and utterly crushed; I groan in anguish of heart. All my longings lie open before you, O Lord; my sighing is not hidden from you. My heart pounds, my strength fails me; even the light has gone from my eyes. My friends and companions avoid me because of my wounds; my neighbours stay far away. Those who seek my life set their traps, those who would harm me talk of my ruin; all day long they plot deception. I am like a deaf man, who cannot hear, like a mute, who cannot open his mouth; I have become like a man who does not hear, whose mouth can offer no reply. I wait for you, O Lord; you will answer, O Lord my God (Ps. 38:3-15).

Look to the Lord and his strength; seek his face always. Remember the wonders he has done, his miracles, and the judgments he pronounced (Ps. 105:4-5).

You guide me with your counsel, and afterward you will take me into glory. Whom have I in heaven but you? And earth has nothing I desire besides you. My flesh and my heart may fail, but God is the strength of my heart and my portion forever (Ps. 73:24-26).

For how can this servant of my lord talk with you, my lord? As for me, no strength remains in me now, nor is any breath left in me. Then again, the one having the likeness of a man touched me and strengthened me. And he said, 'O man greatly beloved, fear not! Peace be to you; be strong, yes, be strong!' (Dan. 10:17-19).

Strengthen the feeble hands, steady the knees that give way; say to those with fearful hearts, 'Be strong, do not fear; your God will come, he will come with vengeance; with divine retribution he will come to save you.' Then will the eyes of the blind be opened and the ears of the deaf unstopped. Then will the lame leap like a deer, and the mute tongue shout for joy. Water will gush forth in the wilderness and streams in the desert. The burning sand will become a pool, the thirsty ground bubbling springs (Isa. 35:3-7).

So do not fear, for I am with you; do not be dismayed, for I am your God. I will strengthen you and help you; I will uphold you with my righteous right hand (Isa. 41:10).

As a shepherd looks after his scattered flock when he is with them, so will I look after my sheep. I will rescue them from all the places where they were scattered on a day of clouds and darkness...will search for the lost and bring back the strays. I will bind up the injured and strengthen the weak (Ezek. 34:11-12).

O Lord my God, I called to you for help and you healed me. O Lord, you brought me up from the grave; you spared me from going down into the pit (Ps. 30:2-5).

Weeping may remain for a night, but rejoicing comes in the morning (Ps. 30:5).

But he was pierced for our transgressions, he was crushed for our iniquities; the punishment that brought us peace was upon him, and by his wounds we are healed (Isa. 53:5).

I am under vows to you, O God; I will present my thank offerings to you. For you have delivered me from death and my feet from stumbling, that I may walk before God in the light of life (Ps. 56:12-13).

Is any one of you sick? He should call the elders of the church to pray over him and anoint him with oil in the name of the Lord. And the prayer offered in faith will make the sick person well; the Lord will raise him up. If he has sinned, he will be forgiven … The prayer of a righteous man is powerful and effective (Jas. 5:13-16).

If we are distressed, it is for your comfort and salvation; if we are comforted, it is for your comfort, which produces in you patient endurance of the same sufferings we suffer (2 Cor. 1:6).

So you shall serve the Lord your God, and he will bless your bread and your water. And I will take sickness away from the midst of you (Ex. 23:25).

Appendix 2

Scriptural Passages of People Healed

Old Testament

Abimelech	Genesis	20:17
Moses' hand	Exodus	4:6-7
Miriam's leprosy	Numbers	12:10-14
Plague on Israelites		16:41-50
Israelites bitten by snakes		21:4-9
Saul's tormented spirit	1 Samuel	16:14-23
King Jeroboam's arm	1 Kings	13:4-6
Widow of Zarephath's son		17:17-24
Shunamite's son	2 Kings	4:8-37
Naaman's leprosy		5:1-14
Hezekiah's illness		20:1-11
Unclean	2 Chronicles	
		30:15-20
Job	Job	1-42
Daniel's troubles	Daniel	4:28-34,36

New Testament

Peter's mother in law	Matthew	8:14-15
Multitudes		8:16-17
Leper		8:2-4

Man with palsy		9:2-8
Man with withered hand		12:9-14
Multitudes		12:15-16
Demoniac		8:28-34
Jarius' daughter		9:18-19,23-26
Woman with bleeding		9:20-22
Sick people		13:58
Multitudes		14:34-36
Syrophoenician's daughter		15:21-28
Child with evil spirit		17:14-18
Blind Bartimaeus		20:29-34
Centurion's servant		8:5-13
Two blind men		9:27-31
Dumb demoniac		9:32,34
Blind and dumb demoniac		12:22
Multitudes		4:23; 9:35; 11:4-5; 14:14; 15:30, 19:2
Blind and lame in temple		21:14
Man with unclean spirit	Mark	1:21-28
Death and dumb man		7:31-37
Blind man		8:22-26
Zechariah's dumbness	Luke	1:18-21,62-64
Widow's son		7:11-17
Mary Magdalene		8:2
Woman bound		13:10-13
Man with dropsy		14:1-4
Ten lepers		17:11-19
Malchus' ear		22:49-51
Multitudes		5:15
Various persons		13:52
Nobleman's son	John	4:46-53
Invalid man		5:1-9

Man born blind		9:1-7
Lazarus		11:1-44
Lame beggar	Acts	3:1-4:22
Aeneas at Lydda		9:32-35
Dorcas at Joppa		9:36:43
Lame man at Lystra		14:8-18
Slave girl at Philippi		14:19-20
Eutchus from dead		20:7-12
Healings in Malta		22:12-21

Essential Survival Guide for the 21st Century

Norman Fisher

ISBN 1-85078-410-8

Which God do we worship?
How do we know what God is like?
The nature of the God we worship.
A loving, caring God?
What's the true nature of man?
Sin, an out-of-date concept or what?
Jesus a man, God, or both?
Jesus rose bodily from death! What does it mean?
What's the Holy Spirit? What about the second coming?
Is the Bible relevant?

This series of studies has been written to answer these questions. After coming to know God we need a helping hand in applying this transformation to our lives and, once we are confident in this, we need to encourage others to do the same.

Written for study over ten weeks, you can go at your own pace, as fast or slow as you like, you can do it with experienced Christians, you can do it on your own, you can use it to help others in their faith, but however you use this resource, its aim is to bring you closer to God and prepare you for your life with Him.

Dr Norman Fisher is Professor of Project Management at The University of Reading UK. He has travelled and lectured extensively around the world. Amongst his interests are boats and fly-fishing. His wife Julia is a writer and a radio presenter and producer. He has two grown up sons.

Seeing it God's Way

Belinda Mackay

ISBN 1-85078-377-2

A challenging and life-changing second book from the author of *China's Dancer*. Belinda Mackay confirms what many of us have long suspected – that our affluent Western lifestyle insulates us from the real needs of so many. And yet …

God has lots of plans to move us out of our comfort zone and into his work. The characters we meet in this book bear witness to what God can do with lives dedicated to serving him and meeting the needs of others.

As we read about the ministry of these people, some famous and some unsung, we are exhorted to put on the mind of Christ; to see things as God sees them. Jesus saw clearly into the hearts and lives of those around him and experienced their hopes, fears and deepest needs.

It's a risky business seeing things God's way. It drives us to prayer, and prayer leads to action. Often he leads us to become the answer to our own prayers. But as he calls us to take risks for him, he meets us at our point of greatest need.

paternoster
Lifestyle

Turning Points
(the booklet)

Vaughan Roberts

ISBN 1-85078-426-4

Is there a meaning to life?

Is human history a random process going nowhere?

Or is it under control – heading towards a goal, a destination?

And what about my life? Where do I fit into the grand scheme of things?

If you're asking these questions, take some time out to think about the answers. Don't walk away from some of the most important discoveries you can explore.

This booklet addresses the issues surrounding the history of man and his purpose as it looks at what the Bible presents as the "turning points" in history, from creation to the end of the world.

Reading this will promise more than thought-provoking discussion but rather help you see history as God sees it, so that you might know how you fit in with His plans for the world, His plans for you.

Vaughan Roberts has worked extensively with students and is Rector of St Ebbe's Church, Oxford.

paternoster
Lifestyle